The Best Made Plans

by

Everett B. Cole

The Best Made Plans
by Everett B. Cole

ISBN: 978-93-59321-74-5

Published by

DOUBLE 9 BOOKS

2/13-B, Ansari Road, Daryaganj
New Delhi – 110002
info@double9books.com
www.double9books.com
Tel. 011-40042856

ABOUT THE AUTHOR

Everett B. Cole (1910-2001) was a professional soldier and a writer of science fiction short tales. He fought at Omaha Beach during WWII and retired in 1960 as a signal maintenance and property officer at Fort Douglas, Utah. He earned a bachelor's degree in math and physics and went on to teach math, physics, and chemistry at Yorktown High School in Texas. In 1951, his debut science fiction story, "Philosophical Corps," appeared in the journal Astounding. Gnome Press published The Philosophical Corps, a reworked version of the story and two others, in 1962. The Best Made Plans, a second novel, was serialized in Astounding in 1959 but never released as a book. He also co-wrote two volumes about the history of south Texas.

Don Michaels twisted about uneasily for a moment, then looked toward the doors of the darkened auditorium. He shook his head, then returned his attention to the stage. Of course, he'd joined in the applause—a guy felt sort of idiotic, just sitting there while everyone else in the place made loud noises—but that comedy act had been pretty smelly. They should have groaned instead of applauding.

Oh, sure, he thought, the drama students had to have experience on the stage. And they really needed an audience—if they were going to have any realism in their performances. Sure, that part of it was all right, but why did the professionals have to join the party? Why did they have to have 'casts like that last thing—especially at a school Aud Call? It seemed anything but educational, and he'd had to skip a good class for this one. He shrugged. Of course, everyone else had skipped one class or another, he knew. So why should he be an exception? Too, some of the students would welcome and applaud anything that gave them a break from their studies. And the schedule probably took account of this sort of thing anyway. But....

A fanfare interrupted his thoughts. From the backstage speakers came the smooth rhythm of a band playing a march trio. He sat back.

The screen glowed and became a large rectangle of blue, dotted with fleecy clouds. In the distance, the towers of Oreladar poked up from a carpet of green trees.

Swiftly, the camera approached the city, to center for a moment on a large sports stadium. Players dashed across the turf, then the camera swung away. Briefly, it paused to record various city scenes, then it crossed the walls of the Palace and came to ground level on the parade grounds of the Royal Guards.

A review was underway. For a few seconds, the camera held on the massed troops, then it centered on the reviewing stand. The band modulated smoothly into a brilliant quickstep and a column of guards marched to center screen, the colors of their dress uniforms contrasting with the green of the perfectly kept field.

Now, the field of view narrowed, centering the view first on the color guard, then on the colors alone. The camera moved down till the gold and blue of Oredan's royal colors stood out against the blue sky.

The band music faded, to be over-ridden then replaced by a smooth baritone voice.

"This is your news reporter," it said, "Merle Boyce, bringing you the latest happenings of the day."

The colors receded, their background blurring then coming into focus again. Now, they stood before a large window. Again, the camera receded and a man appeared in the foreground. For a moment he sat at his plain desk, gazing directly out of the screen and seeming to look searchingly into Don's face. Then he smiled engagingly and nodded.

"As every citizen of Oredan knows," he said, "this nation has been swept by a wave of terrorism during the few days past. Indeed, the now notorious Waern affair became so serious that our Prime Minister found it necessary to take personal command of the Enforcement Corps and direct the search for the terrorists himself. Now, he is present, to bring to you, the people, his report of the conclusion of this terrible affair." He paused, drawing a breath.

"Citizen of Oredan," he declaimed slowly, "the Prime Minister, Daniel Stern, Prince Regent."

He faced away from the camera and faded from view. Again, the gold and blue of Oredan filled the screen.

There was a brief blare of trumpets. Then drums rolled and the heavy banner swept aside to reveal a tall, slender man, who approached the camera deliberately. He glanced aside for a moment, then pinned his audience with an intense stare.

"This has been a terrible experience for many of our people," he began. "And it has been a harrowing time for your public officials. One of our own—a one-time police commissioner—a man sworn to uphold law and order, has suddenly revealed himself as a prime enemy of the realm and of our people. This in itself is a bad thing. But this was not enough for Harle Waern." He held out a hand, his face growing stern.

"No, Waern was unwilling to abide by the results of a lawful trial, knowing the outcome of any full investigation into his activities, he chose to lash out further at authority and to burn his way out of detention. He killed some of his guards. He released other criminals. He formed them into a gang, enlisting their aid in cutting and burning his way across our land in an obvious effort to reach the hills and possibly stir some of the mountain clans to rebellion. And as he went, he left destruction and death." He nodded his head sadly.

"Yes, it is painful to report, but it must be admitted that no less than twenty innocent people have lost their lives as a result of Waern's actions. And many more have been injured or have suffered property loss. It has been a savage affair—one we'll be long in forgetting. And it is with considerable relief that we can report its final conclusion." He stepped back, then faded from view.

The screen brightened again to show a rambling white house which nestled in a grove of shade trees. Behind it, rose a small hill which acted as a mere step toward the peaks of high mountains beyond. Before it was a broad lawn, dotted with lounging furniture. Reflected in its windows was the glow of the rising sun, which flood-lit the entire scene. From the speakers came muted sounds. An insect chirped. Hurrying footsteps crunched on gravel. There were soft rattles and bangs, and somewhere a motor rumbled briefly, then coughed to silence.

"We are now," said a voice, "a few miles outside of the city of Riandar, where Harle Waern had this summer estate built for him."

As the announcer spoke, the camera moved about to pick out details of the estate. It showed a swimming pool back of the house. It swung briefly about landscaped gardens, scanning across cultivated fields and orchards. It flicked across a winding, tree-lined road, then came back to a rough area before the smooth lawn.

Partially concealed from the house by waving grass and field weeds, men were moving cautiously about the fields. Near a small hummock, a loudspeaker rose from its stand, to face the house. A man lay not too far from the base of the stand. Microphone in hand, he looked intently through the grass, to study the windows of the house. Then he glanced back to note the positions of the others.

The camera's viewpoint raised, to take in the entire scene beyond the field. The sky blurred, then seemed to open, to show Daniel Stern's long, thin face. He cast his eyes down for a moment, seeming to take in the details of the scene, then stared straight at the audience, his deep-set eyes glowing hypnotically.

"Here then," he said slowly, "is one of the properties which Harle Waern bought while acting as Police Commissioner of Riandar. Here is a mere sample of the gains he enjoyed for a time as the price of his defections from his oath of office. And here is the stage he chose for the final act, his last struggle against the nation he had betrayed."

His face faded from view, the deep-set eyes shining from the sky for a time after the rest of the face had faded from view.

Then the camera swung again, to show a low-slung weapons carrier which had pulled up a few dozen meters back of the man with the microphone. About it, the air shimmered a little, as though a filmy screen lay between vehicle and camera. It softened the harsh lines of the carrier and its weapon, lending them an almost mystical appearance.

The crew chief was clearly visible, however. He was making adjustments on one of the instruments on the projector mount. One of the crew members stood by on the charge rack, busying himself with adjustments on the charge activators. None of the crew looked toward the camera.

The loud-speaker clicked and rasped into life.

"Harle Waern, this is the Enforcement Corps. We know you are in there. You were seen to go into that house with your friends. You have one minute to throw out your weapons and come out with your hands in the air. This is your last chance."

There was another click from the loud-speaker. Then the scene was quiet.

Someone cleared his throat. The man with the microphone shifted his position and lay stretched out. He had sought cover behind the hummock near the speaker stand and now he raised his head cautiously, to watch the silent windows of the house. Other men lay in similar positions, their attention on the windows, their weapons ready. The windows stared blankly back.

The camera shifted back to the weapons carrier. A low voice spoke.

"Let's have a look at that scope, Walton."

A man's back moved aside and the light and dark pattern of the range detector showed on the screen. The low voice spoke again.

"Four of them," it said. "Looks as though they've got a small arsenal in there with 'em. See those bright pips?"

"Khroal?" queried another voice.

"A couple of those, yeah," the first voice said. "But that isn't too bad. Those are just antipersonnel. They've got a pair of rippers, too. Good thing we've got screens up. And there's a firebug. They could give those guys on the ground a real hard time." A finger appeared in front of the detector.

"See that haze with the lines in it?"

"Them the charges?"

"That's right. They show up like that on both scopes, see? You can always spot heat-ray charges. They look like nothing else. Only trouble is, they louse up the range scale. You can't tell — —"

Don looked critically at the carrier.

There was, he thought, evidence of carelessness. No deflector screens were set up. A Moreku tribesman could put a stone from a sling in there, and really mess them up—if he could sneak in close enough. He grinned inwardly.

"Of course, if he hit the right spot, he'd go up with 'em," he told himself. "Be quite a blast."

He continued to study the weapons carrier arrangements, noting that the chargers were hot, ready for instant activation. Even the gun current was on. He could see the faint iridescence around the beam-forming elements. He shook his head.

"Hit that lens system against something right now," he muttered inaudibly, "or get something in the field, and that would be the end."

The loud-speaker clicked again and the camera swung to center the house in its field of view.

"Your time is running out, Waern." The amplified roar of the voice reverberated from the hills. "You have twenty seconds left."

Abruptly, the speaker became a blaze of almost intolerable light. The man near it rolled away hurriedly, dropping his microphone. Another man quickly picked up a handset and spoke briefly into it.

Again, the camera picked up the weapons carrier. The crew chief had his hand on his microphone switch. He nodded curtly and adjusted a dial. The lens barrel of the projector swung toward the house, stopped, swung back a trifle, and held steady.

The pointer, sitting in front of the crew chief, moved a hand and flicked a switch.

"Locked on."

The crew chief glanced over the man's shoulder, reached out to put his hand on a polished lever, and pressed. Mechanism at the rear of the long projector clicked. The faint glow over the beam formers became a blaze. A charge case dropped out and rolled into a chute. Another charge slid in to replace it and for a brief instant, a coruscating stream of almost solid light formed a bridge between house and carrier.

Then the busy click of mechanism was drowned by the crash of an explosion. A ragged mass of flame shot from the house, boiled skyward, then darkened, to be replaced by a confused blur of smoke and flying debris. The crew chief took his hand from the lever and waited.

At last, the drumroll of echoes faded to silence — the debris fell back to ground — the smoke drifted down the valley with the light breeze. And the rising sun again flooded its light over the estate.

The rambling white house, shaded by its miniature grove of trees, had gone. Charred timbers reached toward the sky from a blackened scar in the grass. On the carefully kept lawn, little red flowers bloomed, their black beds expanding as the flaming blossoms grew.

Near the charred skeleton of the house, one tree remained stubbornly upright, its bare branches hanging brokenly. About it, bright flames danced on the shattered bits of its companions.

In the fields about the house, men were getting to their feet, to stretch cramped muscles and exercise chilled limbs. A few of them started toward the ruins and the man by the speaker got to his feet to wave them back.

"Too hot to approach yet," he shouted. "We'll let a clean-up crew go over it later."

The scene faded. For an instant, the royal colors of Oredan filled the screen, then the banner folded back and Daniel Stern faced his audience, his gaze seeming to search the thoughts of those before him.

"And so," he said, "Harle Waern came to bay and elected to shoot it out with the Enforcement Corps." He moved his head from side to side.

"And with the armament he had gathered, he and his companions might even have succeeded in burning their way to the mountains, despite the cordon of officers surrounding their hide-out. He thought he could do that. But precautions had been taken. Reinforcements were called in. And such force as was needed was called into play." He sighed.

"So there's an end. An end to one case. An end to a false official, who thought he was too big for the law he had sworn to uphold." He held out a hand.

"But there still remain those who hired this man—those who paid him the price of those estates and those good things Waern enjoyed for a time. Your Enforcement Corps is searching for those men. And they will be found. Wherever they are—whoever they are—your Enforcement Corps will not rest so long as one of them remains at liberty." He stared penetratingly at the camera for a moment, then nodded and turned away.

The musical salute to the ruler sounded from the speakers as the scene faded. Once again, the green grass of the Royal Guard parade field came into view. As the color guard stood at attention, the band modulated into the "Song of the Talu."

Don Michaels got out of his seat. The Aud Call would be over in a few minutes, he knew, and he'd have to be at his post when the crowd streamed out. He moved back toward the doors, opened one a trifle, and slid through.

Some others had already come out into the hall. A few more slid out to join them, until a small group stood outside the auditorium. They examined each other casually, then scattered.

Unhurriedly, Don walked through the empty corridors, turning at a stairwell.

How, he wondered, did a man like Harle Waern get started on the wrong track? The man had been a member of one of the oldest of the noble families — had always had plenty of money — plenty of prestige. What was it that made someone like that become a criminal?

"Should've known he'd get caught sooner or later," he told himself, "even if he had no honesty about him. I don't get it."

He got to the bottom of the stairs and walked into the boy's locker room.

Between a couple of rows of lockers, a youth sat in an inconspicuously placed chair. Don went up to him.

"Hi, Darrin," he said. "About ready to pack it up?"

The other gathered his books.

"Yeah. Guess so. Nothing going on down here. Wonder why they have us hanging around this place anyway?"

Don grinned. "Guess somebody broke into a locker once and they want a witness next time. Got to have something for us Guardians to do, don't they?"

"Suppose so. But when you get almost through with your pre-professional ... hey, Michaels, how did you make out on the last exam? Looked to me as though Masterson threw us a few curves. Or did you get the same exam? Like that business about rehabilitation? It ain't in the book."

"Oh, that." Don shrugged. "He gave us the low-down on that during class last week. Suppose your group got the same lecture. You should've checked your notes."

Darrin shrugged and stood up. "Always somebody don't get the news," he grumbled. "This time, it's me. I was out for a few days. Oh, well. How was the Aud?"

Don spread his hands. "About like usual, I'd say. Oh, they had a run on the end of the Waern affair. Really fixed that bird for keeps. Otherwise?"

He waved his hands in a flapping motion.

The other grinned, then turned as a bell clanged.

There was a rumbling series of crashes, followed by a roar which echoed through the corridors. Darrin turned quickly.

"I'd better get going," he said, "before I get caught in the stampede. Should be able to sneak up the back stairs right now. See you later." He strode away.

Michaels nodded and sat down, opening a notebook.

Students commenced rushing into the locker room and the roar in the hall was almost drowned out by the continuous clash and slam of locker doors. Don paid little attention, concentrating on his notes.

At last, the noise died down and Don looked up. Except for one slender figure, crouched by an open locker, the room was empty.

Don looked at the boy curiously. He was a typical Khlorisana—olive skinned, slightly built, somewhat shorter than the average galactic. Don looked with a touch of envy at the smooth hairline, wondering why it was that the natives of this planet always seemed to have a perfect growth of head fur which never needed the attention of a barber. He rubbed his own unruly hair, then shrugged.

"Hate to change places with Pete Waern now, though," he told himself. "Wonder where he stands in this business."

Hurrying footsteps sounded in the corridor and three latecomers rushed in. As Waern straightened to close his locker door, the leader of the group crashed into him.

"Hey," he demanded, "what's the idea trying to trip me?" He paused, looking at the boy closely. "Oh, you again! Still trying to be a big man, huh?" He placed a hand on Waern's chest, pushing violently.

"Out of our way, trash."

Pete Waern staggered back, dropping his books. A notebook landed on its back and sprang open, to scatter paper over the floor. He looked at the mess for an instant.

One of the three laughed.

"That's how you show 'em, Gerry."

Pete stared angrily at his attacker.

"What do you think you're doing?"

The three advanced purposefully. One seized Pete by an arm, swinging him about violently. Another joined him and between them, they held the smaller lad firmly.

Gerry swung an open hand jarringly against Pete's face.

"Guess you're going to have to have a little lesson in how to talk to your betters," he snarled. He drew back a fist.

Don Michaels had come out of his chair. He strode over to the group, to face the attacker.

"Just exactly what *do* you think you're doing?" he demanded icily.

"Who do you think you are?"

Don touched a small bronze button in his lapel. "I'm one of the guys that's supposed to keep order around this place," he said. "We've got self-government in this school, remember?" He swung about to confront the two who still held Waern.

"Now, suppose you turn this guy loose and start explaining yourselves."

Gerry placed a large hand on Don's shoulder, kneading at the muscles suggestively.

"Look, little man," he said patronizingly, "you'll be a lot better off if you just mind your own business. Like watching those lockers over there so they don't fly away or something. We'll take — —"

Michaels swung around slowly, then put knuckles on hips and stared at the other sternly.

"Take that hand away," he said softly. "Now get over there, and start picking up those books. Get them nice and neat." His voice rose a trifle.

"Now, I said!" He stabbed a finger out.

The boy before him hesitated, his face contorted with effort. He forced a hand part way up.

Don continued to stare at him.

The other drew a sobbing breath, then turned away and knelt by the scattered books and papers.

Don wheeled to confront the other two.

"Get over by those lockers," he ordered. "Now, let's hear it. What's your excuse for this row?"

"Aw, you saw it. You saw that little gersal trip Gerry there." The two had backed away, but now one of them started forward again.

"Come to think of it, you don't look so big to me." He half turned.

"Come on, Walt, let's — —"

"Be quiet!" Michaels' gaze speared out at the speaker.

"Now, get over to those lockers. Move!" He swiveled his head to examine the boy who had picked up the books.

"Put them down there by the locker," he said coldly. "Then get yourself over there with your pals." He took a pad and pencil from his pocket, then pointed.

"All right. What's your name?"

"Walt ... Walter Kelton."

"Class group?"

"Three oh one." The boy looked worried. "Hey, what you——"

"I'll tell you all about it—later." Don scribbled on the top sheet of the pad, then tore it off. He pointed again.

"What's your name?"

"Aw, now, look. We——"

"Your name!"

"Aw ... Gerald Kelton."

"Class group?"

"Aw, same as his. We're brothers."

"What's the number of your class group?"

"Aw ... well, it's three oh one. Like I said——"

"Later! Now you. What's your name and class group?"

"Maurie VanSickle. I'm in three oh one, too."

Don finished writing, then snapped three shots of paper toward the three.

"All right. Here are your copies of the report slips. You're charged with group assault. You'll report at the self-government office before noon tomorrow. Know where it is?"

"Yeah. Yeah, we know where it is, all right," grumbled Gerry Kelton. He pointed at Pete Waern.

"How about him?"

"Never mind about that. Just get your stuff and get to your classes. And you better make it fast. Late bell's about to ring. Now get going." Don turned toward Pete Waern.

"Close your locker, fella, and come over here."

He glanced at the three retreating backs, then turned and went back to his chair. Pete hesitated an instant, then picked up his books and locked the door of his locker. Again, he hesitated, and went slowly over to stand in front of Michaels.

Don looked at him curiously.

"You ever have any trouble with those three before now?"

Pete shook his head. "Not really," he said. "Oh, one of the Keltons ... Gerry ... sneaked off the grounds a few weeks ago. I wrote him up." He grinned.

"Pushed on past me when I was on noon guard. I trailed him to his class group later and got his name."

Don nodded. "He ever say anything to you about it?"

"No. I've seen him in the halls a few times since then. He always avoided me—up to now."

"I see." Don nodded. "But today, he suddenly went for you—with reinforcements."

Pete grinned wanly. "I guess I'll have to get used to things like that," he said. "Ever since Uncle Harle was——" He clasped his hands together, then turned suddenly aside.

For an instant, he stood, head averted, then he ran over to lean against a row of lockers, facing away from Michaels.

"Uncle Harle didn't—— Oh, why don't you just leave me alone?"

Don considered him for a moment, then walked over, to place a hand on his shoulder.

"Hey, hold up a minute, Chum," he said. "I'm not trying to give you a bad time. Now suppose you calm down a little. Doesn't do you a bit of good to tear yourself apart. You're not responsible for whatever your uncle got into, you know."

Pete faced him, his back braced against the lockers.

"That's what you say here," he said bitterly. "Sure, we've been in the same classes. You know me, so you try to be decent. But what do you really think? And how about everyone else? You think they're being all nice and understanding about this?" He snorted.

"Know why I'm not in class now? Got no class to go to. I was in Civics Four this period. They threw me out. Faculty advisor said I'd do better in ... in some Shop Study."

Don frowned. "Funny," he said. "You always got good grades. No trouble that way?"

"Of course not." Pete spread his hands. "I——"

A low snicker interrupted the words and Don looked around, to see Gerry Kelton close by. Behind him were his brother and Maurie. Gerry laughed derisively.

"Go ahead," he commented, "let him talk. You might learn something from the little——"

Don motioned impatiently with his head.

"Get going, you three," he said sharply. "You've got less than a minute before late bell."

"Sure we have," Gerry told him. "We might even be late to class. Now wouldn't that be awful? Some jerk wants to write up a bunch of lousy report slips, make him look good, we're — —"

"Move!" Michaels' voice rose sharply. "Don't try that one on me. It's been tried before. Doesn't work."

Gerry paused in mid-stride, then seemed to deflate. He turned away.

"Come on, guys," he said. "Let's get out of here. We'll take care of this later."

As the three disappeared down the hall, Don turned back. Pete was staring at him curiously.

"How do you do that?"

"Do what?"

"Oh, you know what I mean." Pete shook his head impatiently. "Make people do things. There's only one of you and three of them. And they're all bigger than you are. Why did they just do what you told them without making a lot of trouble?"

Don shrugged, then touched the button in his lapel.

"They were in the wrong and they knew it. They've got enough trouble now. Why should they look for more?"

Pete shook his head again. "They didn't have to give their names," he said. "All you did was tell them to."

"What else could they do? After all, you know who Gerry is. So he had no out."

Pete laughed wryly. "Who'd take my word? Besides, Gerry's shoved guardians around before. He's got friends all over school. Ever hear of the 'Hunters'?"

"Who hasn't? Supposed to be some sort of gang, but I've never talked to anyone that knew much about who they are, or what they do." Don was thoughtful. "Supposed to be all galactic kids. I've heard the police are trying to break them up. Those three part of that bunch?"

Pete nodded wordlessly.

Don's eyebrows rose a little. "Prove that," he remarked, "and it won't just be the school that'll be giving them trouble. The police would probably give a lot to really get their hands on some of them."

"I'm not so sure about that," Pete told him. "It was my uncle who was interested in the Hunters. Now, it's different. Maybe the guy that went and got the proof of their membership would be the one who'd have the trouble. Real, final type trouble."

"What's that?"

"Look, I just told you. Among other things, my uncle was interested in the Hunters." Pete bent his knees and took a squatting position. His elbows rested on his knees and he relaxed, resting his chin on folded hands and looking up at Don.

"Seems as though some other people didn't like to have him asking too many questions around." He paused.

"You think my uncle was getting a lot of money from the gamblers and some smuggling combine. That right?"

"Well — —" Don hesitated.

"Sure you do. So does everybody else. The galactics are telling each other about why don't they get somebody in authority besides some stupid Khlorisana. And the Khlorisanu talk about the old nobility — how they can't stop robbing the people. It all goes along with what the papers have been saying. There's been more, too, but those bribery charges are what they've really worked on. They keep telling you some of the same stuff on the newscasts. And everybody believes them. But it isn't true. My uncle was an honest policeman. They got him out of the way because he wouldn't deal with them — and maybe for...." He held out a hand.

"Figure it out. Why didn't they just give him a trial and put him into prison if he were guilty? Or, if they were going to have an execution, why not make it legal — over in Hikoran?" He paused, then waved the hand as Don started to speak.

"They didn't dare have a trial. It would be too public, and there was no real evidence. So they say he escaped. They say he slugged a guard — took his weapons. And he's supposed to have shot his way out of Khor Fortress, after releasing some other prisoners. They say he forced his way clear from Hikoran to the Doer valley." He laughed bitterly.

"Did you ever see Khor Fortress?

"And you should have seen my uncle. He was a little, old man. He'd stand less chance of beating up some guard and taking his weapons than I would have of knocking out all three of those fellows a few minutes ago." Again, he paused, looking at Don searchingly.

"I don't know why I'm telling you all this, unless maybe I better tell someone while I'm still around to talk," he added.

"Now wait." Don shook his head. "Aren't you making — —"

"A great, big thing? No." Pete shook his head decidedly. "I've talked to my uncle. I've heard my uncle and father talk about things. And ... well, maybe I've gotten mixed up in things a little, too. Maybe I'm really mixed up in things, and maybe— —" He stopped talking suddenly and got to his feet.

"No, my uncle didn't escape. That whole affair was staged, so they wouldn't have to bring him to trial. Too many things would have come out, and they could never make a really legal case. This way ... this way, he can't talk. No one can defend him now, and no one will ask too many questions." He turned away.

"Oh, listen." Don was impatient. "That flight developed into a national affair. All kinds of witnesses. It was spread out all over the map. People got killed. Who could set up something like that and make it look genuine?"

Pete didn't look around.

"Look who got killed. A lot of old-line royalists," he said shortly. "And some of the Waernu. You think my uncle would kill his own clansmen?" He expelled an explosive breath.

"And there's one man who could set up something like that. He doesn't like the old royalists very well, either. And he hates the Waernu. Think it over." He walked quickly out of the room.

Don looked after him for a few seconds, then sat down and fixed an unseeing gaze on the far wall of the locker room.

"Gaah!" he told himself, "the kid really pulled the door open. Wonder why he picked me?"

Come to think of it, he wondered, why was it people seemed to tell him things they never mentioned to anyone else? And why was it they seemed to get a sort of paralysis when he barked at them? He scratched an ear. He couldn't remember the time when the ranch hands hadn't jumped to do what he wanted—if he really wanted it. The only person who seemed to be immune was Dad. He grinned.

"Imagine anyone trying to get the Old Man into a dither—and getting away with it."

He laughed and looked at the wall for a few more seconds, then opened a book.

"Wonder," he said to himself. "Seems as though anyone should be able to do it—if they were sure they were right." Then he shook his head. "Only one trouble with that idea," he added. "They don't." He shrugged and turned his attention to the book in his hands.

The click of heels on the flooring finally caused him to look up. He examined the new arrival, then smiled.

"Oh, hello, Jack."

"Hi, Don." The other looked at the array of books. "You look busy enough. Catching up on your skull-work?"

"Yeah. Guy has to study once in a while, just to pass the time away. Besides, this way, the prof doesn't have to spend so much money on red pencils."

"Yeah, sure." Jack Bordelle grinned. "Be terrible if he went broke buying red leads. I go to a lot of trouble myself to keep that from happening." He paused, looked sideways at Don, then rubbed his cheek.

"Speaking of trouble, I hear you had a little scrape here at the beginning of the period."

"That right? Where'd you get that word?"

"Seems as though Gerry Kelton didn't make it to class in time. Teacher ran him out for a late slip and he got me to write him up. He's pretty sore."

Don frowned. "Funny he'd need a late slip. He already had a write-up." He shrugged. "Oh, well. I should get excited about making some of the lower school crowd sore?"

Bordelle lifted one shoulder. "Well, Michaels, you know your own business, I guess, but Kelton's got a lot of friends around, they tell me."

"Yeah. I've heard." Don looked steadily at the other.

"And, well——" Bordelle examined the toes of his shoes carefully. "Well, maybe you ought to think it over about turning in those slips you wrote up, huh?"

"Think so?"

"Well, I would." Bordelle looked up, then down again. "You know, I've known a few guys, crossed the Keltons. Right away, they found themselves all tangled up with the Hunters. Makes things a little rugged, you know?"

"A little rugged, huh?"

"Yeah." Bordelle spread his hands. "Look, Michaels, I've got nothing in this one. It's just ... well, I've known you for a few years now — ever since Lower School. Been in some classes with you. And you seem like a pretty decent, sensible guy. Hate to see you walk into a jam, see? Especially over some native kid with a stinking family record." He paused.

"Of course, it's your own business, but if it were me, I'd tear up those slips, you know?"

"Easy to tear up slips. Only one trouble. They're numbered. How would you explain the missing numbers?"

"Well, guys lose books now and then, remember? Maybe they wouldn't holler too loud."

Don smiled. "I knew a guy once that lost a book. They took it pretty hard. Got real rough about it."

Bordelle shrugged. "Yeah. But maybe Al Wells might not be so rough about it this time, huh? He might just sort of forget it, if you told him you just sort of ... well, maybe you were checking the incinerator on your way to the office, and the book slipped out of your pocket—you know?"

"You think it could happen that way?"

"It could—easy."

Don stood up.

"Tell you," he said, "I might lose a book some day. But they don't come big enough to make me throw one away." He picked up his books and put them under his arm.

"I'm going to turn those slips in tonight. Maybe you'd better turn in the one you wrote up, too. Then nobody'll get burned for losing a book."

"I always thought you were a pretty sensible guy, Michaels." Bordelle shook his head. "After all, you stopped that beef. Nobody got hurt, and you've got nothing to prove about yourself. Know what I mean? So why the big, high nose all at once?"

A bell clanged and the crash and roar of students dashing about echoed through the halls. Don shrugged carelessly.

"Oh, I don't know. Can't even explain it to myself. Maybe I just don't like people pushing other people around. Maybe I don't like to be threatened. Maybe I've even got bit by some of those principles Masterson's always talking about. I don't know." He turned away.

"Well, this is the end of my school day. See you."

Bordelle looked after him.

"Yeah," he said softly. "It's the end of your day all right. Better look out it doesn't turn out to be the end of all your days."

Don glanced down at his textbook, then looked out the window. A blanket of dark clouds obscured the sky. Light rain filtered coldly down, to diffuse the greenery of the school grounds, turning the scene outside into a textured pattern of greens, dotted here and there with a reddish blur. To the west, the mist completely hid the distant mountains.

It would be cold outside—probably down around sixteen degrees or so. It had dropped to fifteen this morning, and unless the weather cleared up, there'd be no point in going up to the hills this weekend. The Korental and his clan would be huddled in their huts, waiting for warmer weather. A wild Ghar hunt would be the last thing they'd be interested in. Besides, the Gharu would be — —

He jerked his attention back to the classroom. A student was reciting.

"... And ... uh, that way, everything was all mixed up with the taxes and the government couldn't get enough money. So King Weronar knew he'd have to get someone to help un ... straighten the taxes out, so he ... uh, well, Daniel Stern had been in the country for a couple of years, and he had ... well, sort of advised. So the king — —"

Don looked out the window again.

With this weather, the ranch would be quiet. Hands would be all in the bunkhouses, crowding around the stoves. Oh, well, he and Dad could fool around down in the range. Since Mom had — — He jerked his head around to face the instructor.

Mr. Barnes was looking at him.

"Um-m-m, yes. That's good, Mara," he said. "Michaels, suppose you go on from there."

Don glanced across at the student who had just finished her recitation, but she merely gave him a blankly unfriendly stare. He looked back at the instructor.

"I lost the last few sentences," he admitted. "Sorry."

Barnes smiled sardonically. "Well, there's an honest admission," he said. "What's the last you picked up?"

Don shrugged resignedly.

"The appointment of Daniel Stern as Minister of Finance," he said. "That would be in eight twelve."

"You didn't miss too much." Barnes nodded. "You just got a little ahead. Take it from there."

"After a few months, the financial affairs of the kingdom began to improve," Don commenced.

"By the middle of eight thirteen, the tax reforms were in full effect. There was strong opposition to the elimination of the old system — both from the old nobility, who had profited by it, and from some of the colonists. But an Enforcement Corps was formed to see that the new taxes were properly administered and promptly paid. And the kingdom became financially stable." He paused.

Actually, he realized with a start, it had been Stern who had founded and trained the Enforcement Corps — first to enforce the revenue taxes, and later as a sort of national police force. And it had always been Stern who had controlled the Enforcement Corps. It was almost a private army, in fact. Maybe Pete — — He continued his recitation.

"Then Prime Minister Delon died rather ... rather suddenly, and the king appointed Mr. Stern to the vacancy. And when King Weronar himself died a little more than four years ago, Prime Minister Stern was acclaimed as prince regent." Don paused thoughtfully.

Delon's death had been sudden — and a little suspicious. But no one had questioned Stern or any of his people about it. And the death of the king and queen themselves — now there was.... Again, he got back to his recitation.

"There was opposition to Mr. Stern's confirmation as Regent, of course, since he was a galactic and not native to the planet. But he was the prime minister, and therefore the logical person to take the reins." He frowned.

"The claims to the throne were — and still are — pretty muddled. No one of the claimants supported by the major tribes is clearly first in line for the throne, and no compromise has been reached." The frown deepened.

"Traditionally," he went on, "the Star Throne should never be vacant for more than five years. So we can expect to see a full conclave of the tribes within a few months, to choose among the claimants and select one to be either head of the clan Onar, or the founder of a new royal line."

Barnes nodded. "Yes, that's fairly clear. But we must remember, of course, that the tradition you mention is no truly binding law or custom. It's merely a superstitious belief, held to by some of the older people, and based on ... well — —" He smiled faintly.

"Actually, under the present circumstances, with no claimant clearly in line, and with the heraldic branch still sifting records, it is far more practical and sensible to recognize the need for a continued regency." He took a step back and propped himself against his desk.

"In any event, most of the claimants of record are too young for independent rule, so the regency will be forced to carry on for some time."

He looked for a fleeting instant at the inconspicuous monitor speaker on the wall.

"As matters stand now, the tribes might find it impossible to decide on any of the claimants. As you said, there is no truly clear line. King Weronar died childless, you remember, and his queen didn't designate a foster son." He shrugged.

"Well, we shall see," he added. "Now, suppose we go back a little, Michaels. You said there was some opposition from the colonists to the tax reforms of eight twelve. Can you go a little more into detail on that?"

Don touched his face. He'd been afraid of that. Somehow, neither the book nor the lectures really jibed with some of the things he'd heard his father talk about. Something about the whole situation just didn't make full sense. He shrugged mentally. Well....

The door opened and a student runner came into the room. Don watched him walk up to Mr. Barnes with some relief. Maybe, after the interruption, someone else would be picked to carry on.

The youngster came to the desk and handed a slip to the instructor, who read it, then looked up.

"Michaels," he said, "you seem to have some business at the self-government office. You may be excused to take care of it."

Al Wells looked up as Don entered the office.

"What's the — — Oh, Michaels. Got some questions for you on that row you stopped in the locker room yesterday."

"Oh? I thought my write-up was pretty clear. What's up?"

The self-government chairman leaned back.

"You said this Gerry Kelton banged into this kid, Waern, started pushing him around, and struck him once. That right?"

Don nodded. "That's about what happened, yes."

"And there was no provocation?"

"None that I saw."

"And you saw the whole affair?"

"Everything that happened in the locker room. Yes."

"Uh huh. And you said that two guys, Walt Kelton and Maurie VanSickle, pinned this kid's arms while Gerry started to slug him. That it?"

Don smiled. "He only got in one slap before I mixed in," he said. "Had his fist all cocked for more, though."

Wells nodded, looking curiously at Don.

"But they quit and turned the kid loose when you told them to?"

"That's right."

"Didn't give you any trouble?"

"No." Don shook his head. "Just some talk. Gave their names and class numbers. Oh, yeah, they squawked a little, sure. Then they took off for class."

Wells looked at Michaels appraisingly.

"Know anything about this Gerry Kelton?"

Don shook his head. "Heard a rumor or so last night," he admitted. "Never heard of him before then."

Wells laughed shortly. "We have. He's only got one year in this school, but we've had him in here several times. Know him pretty well by now. He got set back quite a bit in Primary, so he's some older than most of the Lower School bunch." He waved a hand.

"Oh, he's a brawler. We know that. But he doesn't start fights. He finishes them."

"He started this one."

"That right? And he quit when you told him to?"

"He did."

"Oh, no. That's not the Kelton. Last guy tried to stop him was out of classes for three days. Took five guys to bring Kelton in here." Wells shook his head.

"Look, we got him in here and he told us his story. The other two came up with the same thing later. Makes sense, too—if you know Kelton. It seems he and his brother ran into this kid, Waern, outside the auditorium right after Aud Call. They were talking about the newscast. And this kid came up and started an argument. Tried to slap Walt. They pushed him off and went on their way. VanSickle went with them. He'd been in the crowd." Wells leaned forward.

"Got four witnesses to that, too, beside the three of them."

Don moved his head indifferently. "I wouldn't know about that. I wasn't there. All I know is what I saw in the locker room."

"Yeah. Yeah, sure. Then, they say they went on down to the locker room, after talking to some other students. When they got there, the Waern kid came flying at them again. Tried to bite and kick. They say you helped Maurie pull him off Gerry, and told 'em you'd take it from there. So they went on to class. They can't figure out where you got the idea of writing them up over it. Didn't know they'd been written up till we sent some guys up and pulled them out of their classes." Wells flipped his hands out, palms upward.

"So there's their story. How about it?"

Don shook his head. "Pretty well worked out. Fits the situation, too. Only one trouble. There's almost no truth in it. Pete Waern made no effort to hit any of those three while I was watching. And I didn't touch any of the four myself."

Wells laughed shortly. "That's what you're telling me. I've got a batch of statements telling the other story."

Don looked at the other for a moment. "Now wait a minute," he said slowly. "Are you trying to tell me what I saw and did?"

Wells shook his head. "Just trying to fill you in. This isn't my problem any more. Dr. Rayson's picked it up. Wants to see you. He's got Mr. Masterson with him and they're waiting for you to show up so they can talk things over with you." He tilted his head.

"I don't know. I've heard about some funny things these Khlorisanu can pull off if they can get a guy's attention for a while. And that kid's the real thing—from way back. Better think things over a little, maybe. See if you can remember any dizzy spells or anything."

"Oh, now check your synchs, Wells." Don waggled his head disgustedly. "I've heard those yarns too—down here. Look. All my life, I've been living on a ranch out in the mountains. Got Khlorisanu all over the place. They work for us up there." He grinned.

"Isn't a thing they can do that you and I can't do, too. They've got no special powers, believe me. I know."

"You'd find it pretty hard to tell that one to Doc Rayson and make it stick," Wells told him. "And he's the guy you've got to talk to." He reached into a basket on his desk and took out a stack of papers.

"Look, I've told you more'n I was supposed to all ready. Suppose you go over and talk to them for a while. They're waiting for you over in room Five."

Don looked at him for a moment, then went out.

He swung about and examined the closed door thoughtfully, then massaged the back of his neck.

"What's wrong with these people?" he asked himself. "Don't they know how to break down a rigged story? Or can't they recognize one when they hear it?"

He crossed the hall.

"I'm Donald Michaels," he told the secretary. "I believe Dr. Rayson wants to see me."

The woman looked at him curiously.

"Oh, yes," she said. "Just a minute."

She got up and went into an inner room. After a moment, she came out and reclaimed her seat behind her desk.

"He's busy right now," she said. "I'll let you know when you can go in."

Don shrugged and sat down in one of the chairs that lined the wall. It wasn't a very comfortable chair.

"The anxious seat," he growled to himself. "Nice, time-tested trick."

There was no reading material at hand, and the walls of the oddly shaped room were blank. He amused himself by directing a blank stare toward the secretary. After a few minutes, she looked up from her work and jerked her head indignantly.

"Stop that," she ordered.

"Stop what?" Don looked innocent.

"Stop staring at me like that."

"Not staring at you," he told her. "I have to look somewhere and the chair faces your way. That's all."

The woman moved her hands. "Well, then face some other way."

"But I'd have to move the chair, and that would disturb your arrangements," Don told her reasonably. He continued his blank stare.

The woman resumed her work, then twitched her shoulders and looked at him resentfully for a few seconds. Finally, she got up and went to the inner office again. Don waited.

Again, she came out.

"They'll see you now," she said.

Don got up.

"Thank you."

He went through the door.

To his right, a man sat behind a wide, highly polished desk. The other was across the room, at a smaller desk. Both looked up as the door opened.

The man to Don's right nodded pleasantly.

"Well, so you're Donald Michaels? I'm Dr. Rayson."

"Yes, sir."

"That's good. Sit down." Rayson waved. "Right over there." He smiled confidently.

"Ah, that's fine. I'm the school psychologist, you know. You have met Mr. Masterson, the self-government faculty advisor, of course?"

Don nodded. "Of course. I'm in one of his classes."

"Well, that's good. Now, how do you feel this morning?"

"Quite well, thank you, sir."

"Well, then, we can talk about that little affair in the locker room, can't we? Your memory is clear on it by now, isn't it?"

Don nodded.

"Well, that's fine. Now, suppose you give us the whole story. Don't leave out a thing. Then, we'll see what we can do for you."

Don smiled thinly, then flicked out a finger.

"I think that paper on your desk, sir, is the report I wrote last night. It's complete as it stands."

Masterson broke in, frowning. "We don't mean that thing," he said coldly. "What we want is a true, complete account of what actually happened."

Don faced him, his face tightening a little.

"Dr. Rayson has just that, sir," he said. "On his desk. I wrote it. I signed it."

Rayson raised a hand slightly.

"Just a moment," he said reprovingly. "There's no need for excitement or anger here. We're simply looking for a full, correct account." He cleared his throat. "Perhaps it would be well for me to make things clearer to you. Then, you'll recognize the problem." He looked down at the paper on the desk.

"You see, Donald," he continued, "we have already talked to a number of other students about this. And we have a complete account of the incident in so far as it concerned Petoen Waern." He smiled indulgently.

"What we are now concerned about is your own well-being. We need to know something of what happened to you after you were alone with the Waern boy." He spread his hands, then held them out, palms up.

"As to the actual physical action, that's quite simple. You see, there were a number of witnesses to the affair, and most of them have come forward." He rubbed his hands together, then laid them on the desk.

"So, we know precisely what happened that far.

"And we have a pretty good idea of what happened to you later, of course. This sort of thing has happened before. But by this time, you should have had time to recover to a great extent. At least, you should remember things much more clearly than you did when you wrote this report last night." He touched the paper with a smile.

"And with a little prompting and information, you should be able to fully recover your memory."

The smile became sympathetic. "Of course, I can understand your present confusion and your complete disbelief in your change of orientation. And I know it's quite an effort for a young man to admit he's been ... well ... shall we say influenced? But believe me, it's no disgrace. It's happened to quite a few others before you." He nodded thoughtfully.

"In fact, we are beginning to believe this Petoen Waern, like his uncle, is something of an adept at this sort of thing."

Don looked at him steadily.

"Do I act as though I were in a trance, sir?"

"Oh no. No, of course not. This sort of thing doesn't result in such a manifestation. This is something much more subtle than mere, gross hypnotism." Rayson smiled.

"However, you've had all night to partially recover. And these things seldom are fully effective for more than a few hours — unless the operator can get to his victim again, to fully fix the impression he has created."

Rayson placed the palms of his hands together. "No, by this time, one would expect your memories to be somewhat confused. So we can apply therapeutic methods." He nodded.

"Now go ahead. Try running through the whole story. Perhaps we can get a clue as to his methods. And if you have any ill effects remaining, I think they can be quite easily eliminated. Now, suppose you start with the time immediately after young Waern's attack on the Kelton boy."

Don shook his head wearily. "There was no such attack," he said. "It was the other way around. A large sized chap who later gave his name to me as Gerry Kelton, slapped a smaller fellow named Waern. At the time, two other fellows were holding Waern's arms. Rather tightly, too."

Masterson interrupted, shaking his head disgustedly. "We've got plenty of statements from witnesses. That isn't the way they read. Now how about it?"

"You mean the two Keltons and VanSickle?"

"No." Masterson was definite. "No. I don't mean them. There were several students around the doorway into that locker room during that entire show. We got stories from most of them." He waved a hand decisively.

"Now suppose you start using your head. Get busy and give us the thing the way it really happened. Then, we'll see what to do about you."

Don shook his head. "The locker room and the hall were empty for at least a full minute before those three came in," he said. "If you go over the people that signed those statements, you'll probably find that they were somewhere else at the time." He grinned.

"And from what I hear, this might give you an idea as to the membership of the Hunters, too."

"Hunters!" Masterson looked completely disgusted. "We've checked out a hundred crazy rumors about that alleged gang. Nothing there."

"Maybe so." Don looked at him critically. "But Jack Bordelle certainly sounded convinced last night. And how about Pete Waern? Didn't he tell you his side of this thing?"

"Ah yes, Waern." Dr. Rayson chuckled. "I believe these 'Hunters' are an invention of his uncle's. No, that young man didn't come in. His father is too smart for that. We won't see that young man again, unless we can have him brought in for this bit of work he did on you."

Don turned his head to stare across the desk.

Rayson smiled knowingly. "Oh, yes. Jasu Waern called early this morning. He said he was withdrawing Petoen from school. Said he planned to send him to a private school where he wouldn't be subject to indignities." He chuckled again.

"Jasu Waern is altogether too smart a man to let us question that youngster of his if he can prevent it." He looked searchingly at Don.

"You know," he added musingly, "I'm beginning to wonder about you, though. This might be serious. Possibly this Waern boy was more thorough than we thought possible. Possibly permanent damage could have been done." He got to his feet.

"Suppose you go over to that couch there and lie down. We'll try a little therapy, and see what we can do for you."

Michaels looked at him indignantly.

"I'm getting a little tired of all these tales about mental influence by the Khlorisanu. They're pure myth and I know it. I've lived all my life among these people. Believe me, if there were any such thing, my father or I would have come across it before now. And we'd know about it."

"You are then, ah, presenting yourself as an authority on parapsychology, perhaps?" Rayson pursed his lips. "This is a great accomplishment for one so young."

"I'm not an authority on anything." Don shook his head. "All I know is that I'd find it out right away if anyone tried anything like that on me. No one has—at least no Khlorisana has."

Rayson shook his head reprovingly. "Now, you say you have lived all your life among these people? Perhaps, then, you have been under——"

"Just a minute!" Masterson broke in sharply. "What's this about Jack Bordelle? He's your relief, isn't he, Michaels?"

"That's right." Don shrugged, then repeated his conversation with Bordelle. He smiled wryly as he finished.

"I'll have to admit," he added, "I did walk over and spend a few seconds checking the incinerator, at that. But ... oh, well." He waved at the paper on Rayson's desk.

"And you didn't put that in your report?"

"No, sir. I didn't think there was any place for it there."

"Why not?"

"It wasn't material to the case in hand, sir. There was no evidence in Jack's comments. He made no threats or offers. And as far as I could tell, he was merely a disinterested person concerned in my welfare. Even though he seemed to believe what he was saying, it's pure hearsay."

"Hearsay!" Masterson snorted. "Pure invention." He leaned forward.

"Look," he said sharply, "we've been pretty patient with you. We've given you the benefit of every doubt we could think of. And we're getting to the time-wasting stage." He waved a hand sharply across in front of his body.

"Now, I'd like to get some truth out of you. You've told us a little truth already. I believe you when you say you weren't subjected to any mental influence. I think the influence was very material indeed—in nice, purple ink—and it seems to have been pretty effective. How much was it?"

"How much?" Don frowned. "I wish you'd make yourself clear on that. What are you trying to say?"

"Just what you think I said," snapped Masterson. "How much did that youngster offer you to write up that incident the way you did? And have you the cash in hand yet?"

Don looked at the man carefully, noting the details of his appearance. Finally, he shook his head.

"Mr. Masterson," he said slowly, "up to now, I've always thought you were a good instructor and a fine advisor. I've sat in your classes, and I even developed a lot of respect for you. All at once, you've shown me how wrong I could be." He held up a hand.

"Be quiet," he said sharply, "both of you. And listen carefully. I want to make myself fully understood. I want to drive one thought into your stupid heads. You're in the wrong part of the galaxy for such remarks as that one you just made." He touched the corner of his mouth, then looked at his fingers.

"You see, this is at the edge of the Morek. There are Moreku here, in this school. And some day, you might talk to one of them." He smiled thinly.

"I am the only son of a border rancher, Mr. Masterson. We have a few thousand square kilos up in the Morek area, in the hills. And I have worked and played with mountain tribesmen all my life." He drew a long breath.

"Had a few fights with some of them, too. And some of their customs and a lot of their moral values rubbed off on me, I guess, though I've never been adopted into any clan.

"You just made a remark that is the absolute last word in insults up in the Morek. Nothing you could do or say could be worse. And there are, as I said, others from that area right here, in this school. Real clan members." He laughed shortly.

"Mister, what you said was, 'you sell yourself.'" He reached up to his lapel, twisting at the bronze button.

"If you should say that to a tribesman, your life would be over. Right then, unless you were very quick. And if you should be quick enough, or lucky enough, to kill the man you insulted, his clan brothers would take it up. It would be either you — or the whole tribe." He stood up.

"I'm not a tribesman. I don't carry the sling, and I'm of galactic ancestry, so I don't have a compulsion toward blood vengeance. But I don't accept that insult. I shall go back to the Morek today and place you out of my mind." He paused.

"No, I won't kill you. I'll simply warn you so you'll have no excuse for such idiocy again." He smiled.

"You know, Mr. Masterson, I don't know how much they pay you by the year to sit around here, but I doubt that it's as much as I pay my beaters for a week end of hunting. So obviously, even if I were for sale, the man who could afford the tab could pick you up with his small change." He paused thoughtfully.

"Come to think of it, if your annual pay is more than my beaters get, I'll have to raise their wages. They do their job — intelligently."

He turned, then swung back for an instant. The bronze button had come out of his lapel. He tossed it on Masterson's desk.

"Here," he said. "A present for you. I can't stand the smell of it."

Dully, the two men sat, watching the closed door. At long last, Rayson turned his head with obvious effort, to stare at Masterson, who recovered a few milliseconds more slowly.

But Masterson's recovery was the more violent of the two. He stared blankly at Rayson for an instant, then sprang to his feet.

"Why that young...! I'll turn him every way but loose."

He sprang around his desk and took a stride toward the door.

"No, no." Rayson raised a hand warningly. "This is no way to handle such a matter." He smiled gently.

"After all, this young man succeeded in immobilizing both of us for a considerable time. In the first place, I doubt you'd be able to catch him. In the second, do you think he would stand still while you mauled him by yourself?"

Masterson turned around, frowning. "He caught me unprepared," he snarled. "He can't do that to me again. Not while I'm ready for him."

"No? I think he could. Any time, any place, and under almost any conditions. And I have much more experience in these matters than you, my friend. This is a very dangerous young man, and he requires special handling. Sit down and let us consider this young man."

Masterson growled impatiently, but returned to his desk. He sat down, glowering at his companion.

"Suppose you tell me what you're talking about," he demanded.

Rayson looked down at his hands, which rested on the desk.

"We have been talking about mental influence, I believe. In fact, we mentioned this very matter to our young friend. This is correct?"

"Sure we did. So?"

"And our young man was quite positive that he could never be so controlled and that any effort to do so would be immediately apparent to him. This is also correct, I believe?"

"That's about the way of it, yes. What are you driving at?"

Rayson sighed. "Let me remind you of something, then. You are, of course; of the Ministerial Investigative Force, just as I am. But our specialties are different. Your dealings are with the teaching and preparation of youth for useful citizenship, and with the prevention of certain gross misbehavior. Thus, you deal with those more obvious and material deviations from the socially acceptable and have little experience with the more dangerous and even less acceptable deviations with which I must concern myself." He smiled faintly.

"Your handling of this young man just now would indicate a quite complete lack of understanding of the specialty I have prepared myself for. And even if there were no other reasons, it would serve to point up the reason for our difference in relative rank. You must admit you got something less than desirable results." He cleared his throat and looked disapprovingly at Masterson.

"Of course, you are familiar with stories of mental influence. And I have no doubt that you have had some experience with this type of thing, even though it is not in your direct line of work."

Masterson shook his head. "Sorry," he admitted. "This is the first time anyone's ever pulled anything like that on me."

Rayson inclined his head slowly. "So," he said softly. "Your lack of caution and discretion is more understandable, then. You have been quite fortunate, I should say. Of course, extreme individualism is far from common now, and persons who combine extreme individualism with high empathic power are rare, but they do appear. And they are dangerous in the highest degree." He spread his hands.

"A fully developed person of this type could do almost as he pleased and there would be no one who would be able to deny him or even check his course. You can see what I mean, surely?"

Masterson stared contemplatively into space. "Yes," he said. "Yes, I think I get the idea. A person like that could demand almost anything from almost anyone—and get it. But how would you go about it to restrain one of those people?"

"It can lead to difficulties." Rayson smiled reminiscently. "I can remember cases where— —" He frowned.

"But no matter. We seldom allow them to reach high development. Very often, they betray themselves in little ways and we discover them quite early. We are then able to take care of them before they can do serious harm. Some, even, we are able to ... ah ... reorient, so that they become normal, useful subjects of the realm. But sometimes ... well, we have to call upon the Guard and get heavy weapons. Complete elimination becomes necessary." He frowned.

"And sometimes, like our young friend, they gain considerable power which they manage to conceal, and only betray themselves when under stress. Then, they become dangerous in the extreme. And there is no really legal way in which they can be handled, since they haven't yet committed any overt act of violence." He shook his head.

"No, this young man will require quite special handling. He will have to be carefully watched, and will probably get to the stage where complete elimination is demanded. I shall set the process in motion immediately." He reached for the telephone on his desk.

Masterson looked at him thoughtfully.

"You say these people are pretty rare, and really dangerous?"

"Yes. To both questions, definitely yes."

"Well, then, I should think that anyone who managed to organize and direct the elimination of one of them would be likely to get quite a bit of credit. Might even lead to a good promotion."

Rayson took his hand from the telephone.

"This is true," he admitted. "You are thinking of — —?"

Masterson nodded. "Why don't we pick up a few people and run this operation ourselves?" he asked.

Rayson shook his head. "The idea is excellent," he agreed. "But I really see no reason for a joint effort." He got to his feet.

"After all, you must admit the total implication of this matter was my discovery. I had to explain it to you. And thus, I can see no reason for making a full partnership of the matter." He raised a hand.

"Of course, you will receive credit in the matter," he added quickly, "and you might even find yourself advanced. But I shall have to insist on taking the final steps and directing the operation personally." He smiled coldly.

"I can consult with certain of my colleagues and get the necessary support. And when I have left, you may get in touch with your superiors and report the matter, telling them that action is being initiated. This way, we will both receive our due credit." He paused.

"Oh, yes," he added, "and you might interview this young Kelton again, with his companions. Thus, you will gather evidence for use in justifying my operations."

Masterson looked at him unhappily. "Well ... all right," he agreed reluctantly. "Rank has its privileges, I suppose. And I guess in this case, that includes the collection of more rank. Suppose I'd better take what I can get."

"To be sure." Rayson smiled at him benignly. "This way, you are sure of profiting. Otherwise, you might run into disaster." He rose and strode toward the door.

"You may get those boys in for interview as soon as I leave," he said. "From them, you can get sufficient evidence of these powers of your young friend. Ah ... and I would suggest that you use a little more discretion with them than you showed with this young Michaels of ours. You were a trifle — shall we say, crude?" He coughed.

"Then you may call in and advise Headquarters that evidence has been gathered and action is being taken in this case of Donald Michaels."

He turned and went out the door.

Masterson watched as the door closed, then reached into the back of a desk drawer. He took out a small box with a number of switches mounted on its top. For a moment, he examined the object, then he got to his feet and went to the window.

He stood, looking out of the window for a few moments, nodded, and let his fingers play among the switches. Finally, he nodded in satisfaction and went back to his desk.

He looked contemplatively at the telephone for a moment, then picked it up and started flipping at the dial.

The sports flier dropped free for the last few feet, bounced, tilted, and finally righted itself. It was not a very good landing.

Don snapped the switch off and sat for a moment, looking out at the long, low house. Then he let himself out of the flier and walked across the courtyard and through the door.

The front room was empty. He looked over at the wide glass panels that formed one side of the room. A small, dark man came from between the bushes of the inner garden. He slid a panel aside and looked expressionlessly at Don for a moment. Then he slowly allowed his head to drop.

"Master Donald," he said. He raised his head, looking at Don with brilliant yellow eyes. "Your father did not expect you until two days."

"I know, Dowro. But I came home early. I want to talk to him."

"It is well." The man motioned toward a curtained arch. "He is below."

"Thanks, Dowro. I'll find him." Don swept the curtains aside and turned, to open a heavy door.

As he started down the steep flight of stairs, a sharp crack came from the basement. He grinned. With this kind of weather, the range would be busy.

Kent Michaels stood on the plastic flooring, a rifle at his shoulder. The front sight weaved almost imperceptibly, then steadied. He seemed completely unaware of his son's presence.

Suddenly, a spurt of smoke came from the muzzle of the rifle. There was another sharp crack and the muzzle swept upward then dropped, to become steady again.

At last, the shooter took the weapon from his shoulder and opened the action. He looked around.

"Oh, Don," he said. "Didn't expect you for a couple of days. There's no holiday down there right now, is there?"

Don shook his head. "I made a new one," he said. "Permanent type."

His father bent over the rifle action, examining it. Then he stepped over to place the weapon in a rack. Finally, he turned, to look searchingly at his son.

"Permanent?"

"Afraid so, Dad. I guess I sort of blew up."

"Want to tell me about it?"

The older man motioned Don to a camp stool and pulled one over for himself. As Don talked, he listened intently. At last, he nodded.

"So that's all of that, eh?"

"Guess it is, Dad. Looks as though I'll have to start working for my keep. Won't be any police official in the family after all."

"Could be." Kent Michaels got up and reached out to the weapons rack.

"Got one more shot on this target. Then we'll talk it over, hm-m-mm?"

He stepped up to a line inlaid in the floor. Deliberately, he placed a cartridge in the rifle and closed the action. Then, he raised the weapon, seated it on his shoulder, and brought it into position with a twisting motion.

Don watched, smiling in spite of himself, as the front sight rose and fell with his father's breathing. That routine never changed. From the time the Old Man picked up his weapon till he laid it down, you could predict every move he'd make.

The motion stopped and for endless seconds, the man stood motionless, the muzzle of his rifle probing steadily toward the lighted space downrange. Then the front sight jumped upward, settled back, and steadied again.

"Looked good." Kent Michaels let the weapon down, opened the action and checked it, then racked the weapon. He touched a button near the firing line and waited for the target to come in to him.

Deliberately, he unclipped the sheet of paper, laid it down, and clipped another in its place. He touched another button, then picked up the fired target and bent over it, checking his score. Finally, he looked up.

"Ninety-seven," he said. "Four X's. Think you can beat it?" He walked back to the rack and picked out a rifle. After glancing into the action, he held it out toward Don.

"Zero hasn't been changed since you fired it last. Want to take a couple of free ones anyway, just to be sure?"

Don looked at him indignantly.

"Good grief, Dad," he objected. "This is no time for a rifle match."

"Good as any, I'd say," his father told him. "Go ahead. There's a block of ammo at the point. Take your time, but you'll have to make 'em good." He sat down on his camp stool and waited.

Don looked at him for a few seconds, then shook his head resignedly and stepped up to the line.

"Oh, well," he said. "I'll try. Never mind the zero rounds."

He loaded the rifle and brought it to his shoulder. The sight weaved and bobbed. He brought it down again and looked back at his father. The older man pulled a cigarette from his breast pocket.

"Go ahead," he said calmly. "Take a few deep breaths. And relax."

Don bowed his shoulders and let the rifle hang loosely from his outstretched arms. He looked downrange, trying to drive everything out of his mind but the target hanging down there. Finally, he raised the weapon again. The sight bobbed about, then steadied. He put pressure on the trigger, then growled softly as the weapon fired.

"Oh, no! Drifted off at three o'clock."

His father exhaled a small cloud of smoke and said nothing. Don looked at him unhappily for a moment, then reloaded and brought the rifle up again.

Finally, the tenth shot smacked against the backstop and he racked his weapon and punched at the target return button.

His father got up and unclipped the sheet.

"Well, let's see," he said. "Eight, nine, nine ... here's a nipper ten ... nine ... oh, me! You didn't do so well, did you?"

"What would you expect?" grumbled Don. "Give me a couple of hours to simmer down and I'll take you on. Beat you, too."

"Suppose you got into a fight, Don?" his father asked. "Think the guy'd give you a couple hours to simmer down? So you could maybe shoot his eye out?"

He turned and led the way to a couple of lounge chairs.

"Sit down," he advised. "And turn on that light, will you?" He leaned back.

"So you gave Andy Masterson a fast outline on manners, eh?" He laughed softly. "Boy, I'd like to have seen his face about then!"

Don jerked his head around. "You know him, Dad?"

"You could say I did once," his father answered. "We went through Guard training together. Served on the same base a few times. Some years ago, I retired. I'm pretty sure he didn't."

Don pushed himself out of the chair and stood in front of his father.

"You mean Mr. Masterson is— —"

Kent Michaels nodded slowly. "Stellar Guard Investigations? Yes, and I suspect he could wear quite a bit of silver lace, too, if he wanted to get dressed up." He clasped his hands behind his head.

"Let's see, Don, you're almost twenty now. Right?"

"That's right, Dad."

"Uh huh. And you were born here on Khloris. Means I've been out of active duty for quite a while, at that." He smiled.

"Got papers upstairs. They say I retired a little more than twenty-one years ago. Got official permission to live on an outworld and joined the first group of colonists here. Of course, they don't say anything about the people that told me to do all that."

Don stared at him. "What are you getting at, Dad?"

His father smiled. "Man retires, he's supposed to be all through with duty. Not subject to recall except in case of galaxy-wide emergency." He nodded thoughtfully.

"True. But a lot of people never really retire from the Guard. Things keep coming up, and that pension begins to look more like a retainer fee."

He held up a hand.

"Suppose I give you a little go-around on some history that isn't in the books—at least not in the books they use in these schools.

"Of course, you know about the arrival of the *Stellar Queen*. You've read all about the original trade contracts here in Oredan. And you've read a lot about the immigrations. And the border settlements.

"Yes, and you know about the accession of Daniel Stern, first to the Ministry of Finance, then to the Prime Ministry, then to the Regency. Quite a success story, that. And you have read about the mixup in the royal succession." He smiled.

"It all went about that way. Oh, sure, it wasn't quite as peaceable and orderly as the books make it look, but no history bothers with the minor slugfests. What they're concerned in is the big picture.

"Well, when the king agreed to colonization of the outer provinces, quite a few people came crowding out here. And there was more than a little thievery and brawling and rioting. Naturally, the Federation Council was interested. And the Stellar Guard was more directly interested.

"So, they encouraged a lot of retired guardsmen to come out here, weapons and all. And they assigned a few more people to … well, sort of keep an eye on things. They set some people up with reasonably decent claims, saw to it that the rest of us got a good start, and left us to take it from there." He smiled.

"We had some fun, now and then. Got the border pacified. Got the crooks and the tough boys calmed down. And we got the hill tribes cooled off some, too. Even made friends with them — after a while. And some guys got married and made noises like real Khlorisanu — genuine Oredanu, in fact. A few of them married Oredana girls." He laughed shortly.

"The Khlorisanu are humanoid — human to as many decimals as you need to go. There's a little minor variation in superficial appearance between them and the average galactic, but there's no basic difference. Quite a few of the fellows found the local girls made good wives.

"But anyway. There wasn't any real organization among us. We just … well, sort of knew what the other fellow was about. Kind of kept our own personal policy files. And things went along pretty well.

"Oh, there were some fellows who stuck to some sort of organizational structure, I suppose. You know how that is — some guys can't draw a deep breath unless the rest of the team is there to fill in the picture.

"And then, there were several people like Andy Masterson, who showed up from nowhere. That was none of my business. Happened to know Andy, but I've never talked to him here. Those people had complete new backgrounds. No Guard experience — it says here. And they joined the economy — took out Oredan citizenship. Some of them got into government work.

"Then this guy, Daniel Stern, showed up. He started grabbing influence with both hands. Smart young guy. Killed off a prime minister — we think — and a king. Can't prove any of that, though." Kent shook his head.

"Don't think we didn't try to stop him, once we realized what he was up to. We did. About that time, a whole lot of us did get together and organize. But he's one of those people. If he tells a man to go out and shoot himself, the next thing you hear is the sound of a falling body." His eyes clouded and he looked searchingly at Don.

"You should know what I mean. Like when you told that Ghar thief to tell us all about it—remember?"

"Look, Dad, that's something I'd like to know...."

Kent Michaels waved a hand. "So would I. But I know less about it than you do, so it's no use. All I know is that some people can tell most anyone to do almost anything—and it gets done. As I said, Stern seems to be one of them." He shrugged.

"Anyway, we lost a lot of good colonists before we decided to sit back and wait this boy out.

"It's been a long wait. Some of us have gotten rich in the meantime, in spite of Stern's trick taxes. Some of us have had a pretty rough time, I guess. But we're all growing older, and Stern's pretty cagey about immigration. Doubt if many guardsmen are getting in these days. We're going to have to depend on our kids, I think."

Don leaned forward.

"In other words, I could have kicked over an applecart?"

"Well, let's say you might have bent an axle on your own pretty, blue wagon. It's a good thing Masterson was there when you blew up. Anyone else, and I might have come up short one son. I wouldn't like that too well. Might make me go down to Oreladar and try a little target practice." He frowned thoughtfully.

"You know, come to think of it, no one ever made me do anything I didn't want to do."

Don looked thoughtful.

"What do I do now?"

"Just what you said. Start working for your keep. If I get the news right, the waiting period is about over. Stern's finally dipped his toe in the water, with that business over Waern, and we might be able to do something. You just might get your teeth into it. And maybe I'll find myself going back to work.

"First, you'll have to go back to Riandar. Apologize to Masterson, of course, and give him a peace offering. I'll give you a bottle of Diamond Brandy before you leave. Be sure you hold the diamond in front of him when you stick the bottle out. Otherwise, he might throw something. He'll take it from there." The older man grinned.

"And if I remember Andy Masterson, he'll come up with enough work to keep you busy."

Andrew Masterson frowned at the bottle held before him.

"What's this?" he inquired. "You know better than to bring stuff like this on the grounds."

Don Michaels shrugged. "Dad said there wasn't too much of it around any more. Thought you might like some."

"Oh, he did? Yeah. Well, I'll take it as well meant. Might find someone who could use it." Masterson opened a drawer and thrust the bottle inside.

"He have anything else to say?"

Don nodded, looking at Masterson's suddenly watchful eyes. "He said if you'd come up our way, he'd show you how to hold 'em and squeeze 'em. Said maybe you might like to bring up some friends some time and give them a chance to find out what border life is like."

"Huh! You mean he's still playing games with those antique lead tossers?" Masterson grinned suddenly. "Thought he'd have outgrown that foolishness years ago. By the way, how's he shooting these days?"

"Fired a pinwheel after I told him about the row yesterday. Meant he only dropped three points on the target — standing."

"So? Maybe he could do damage with one of those antiques of his, at that — if he could get someone to hold still long enough for him to shoot at them. But nobody makes ammunition for the things any more. Where's he getting that?"

"Makes it himself." Don smiled. "He's got quite a workshop down in the basement."

Masterson nodded. "That's Kent Michaels, all right. O.K., youngster, I knew who you were in the first place. Just checking. Tell me, did he get you mixed up with that antique craze of his?"

Don nodded. "I beat him at it once in a while, sir."

"Did you hand him another beating yesterday? When you went out of here, it looked as though you were going to have to whip somebody."

Don frowned. "He made a monkey out of me. I couldn't stay on target."

"Uh, huh." Masterson nodded slowly. "Figures. Remember that, that it'll be the most valuable match you ever lost."

"Sir?"

"That's right. Yesterday, you got pretty well charged up. Even managed to warm up a secret police agent. Doesn't pay, believe me. About the time you get emotionally involved in a problem, the problem turns around and bites you. You're lucky. Someone else got bit instead—this time. You see, one of us didn't get shook up."

"I don't——"

Masterson tilted his head. "We had an unfortunate accident here right after you left. Dr. Rayson went rushing out of here and took off in his flier. Something went wrong—nobody's sure what. Maybe he didn't let his stabilizing rotors have time to lock in. Maybe a lot of things. Anyway, he flipped about fifty meters up. Came down pretty fast, and burned right by the parking lot. Quite a mess." He nodded sadly.

"Shame. Fine psychologist, and one of the best secret policemen in the realm."

"You——"

Masterson held up a hand. "Let's just say he was careless." He motioned.

"Sit down. No, not in the hot seat. Take that one over there. Then you can see things." He drew a long breath.

"Your father say anything about Stern?"

Don nodded. "He doesn't like him too well."

"He's got company. Know what Stern's trying to do, don't you?"

Don laughed uneasily. "I'm pretty well mixed up, to be truthful. From what Dad told me, he's trying to turn Oredan into a Dictatorship, with him at the head. Then, he'll take over the rest of the planet—a piece at a time."

"Close. He's planned it pretty well, too. He's got the royal succession pretty well balled up. He's almost ready to move in right now. Only one stumbling block. Know what that is?"

Don shook his head.

"Youngster named Petoen Waern. He's old enough—older than he looks. His mother's a niece of the last king. Conclave of the tribes could put him on the throne tomorrow morning. He's a bet Stern missed a while back. Now, he's trying to make up for it."

Don frowned. "Is that really why——"

"Right. That's why the row in the locker room. That would have eliminated that claimant in a hurry. Nobody wants a king with a family criminal record and a habit of starting brawls—especially when he loses those brawls. Kings just aren't supposed to go in for that sort of thing." Masterson smiled mirthlessly.

"Anyway, I doubt he'd have survived that affair if you hadn't rammed your neck into it."

"But there are other claimants. They'll come of age pretty soon."

"Sure they will. But that's pretty soon — and not soon enough. Besides, Stern's got them under control, along with their families — the important ones, anyway. There'd be a deadlock when a conclave started checking their claims. And somehow, their councilors wouldn't be able to come up with quite the right arguments."

"If a formal conclave meets, and no claimant is clearly eligible for the throne — know who'll be called to start a new royal line?"

"But he— —" Don shook his head doubtfully.

"Yes, he could." Masterson shook his head. "Sure, he's regent. But he hasn't renounced his position as prime minister. And with his personal effect on people, he couldn't lose. No, the only reason he can't stand a conclave right now is one youngster — and one family he's never been able to control, because they stay out of his personal reach. And he almost got the youngster out of the way. Neat little operation, with only one thing that could go wrong. You."

Don frowned. "But that affair was just a personal— —"

"Think so? Oh, sure, I gave the Hunters a big horselaugh yesterday. Rayson was around then. And Rayson was a pretty big boy. He knew all about the Hunters, I'm pretty sure. And I know better than to laugh about them." He leaned forward.

"I can't prove it, and it wouldn't do too much good if I tried, but I know perfectly well who's behind not only the Hunters, but a flock of other criminal gangs — juvenile and adult as well. Think I didn't know I was talking to a bunch of Hunters when I listened to that rigged story of theirs about the Keltons? Think I didn't realize Rayson was sitting there prompting them whenever they started to get confused?" He smiled.

"Maybe I'm stupid, but I'm not that stupid. The reason I was rough on you was the fact I didn't want you signing any statements that Pete had hypnotized — or what would you call it — you. That would have fixed the whole thing and they'd have had him." He coughed.

"And, too, I knew who you were, of course. I didn't know for certain how you stood, or how much you could do, but you looked good. And it was pretty obvious you had capabilities." He smiled.

"Some of the retired guardsmen have had sons go sour on them, you know, so I can't take 'em just on faith. But, as I said, the locker room deal looked good, and the more you talked, the better I liked it."

"But you — —"

"Yeah, I know. I wasn't taking such a chance, though, at that. Truth of the matter is I'm about as bad as your father. You couldn't make me give you the right time if I didn't feel like it." Masterson's eyes crinkled in an amused smile.

"Go ahead. Try it."

Don shook his head. "I'll take your word," he said. "I tried to tell Dad off once. Somehow, things get a little unpleasant."

"Yeah." Masterson stretched luxuriously. "Anyway, I figured you'd be a lot handier around here alive and in operating condition. The last thing I could let happen would be for Rayson to get you on that trick table of his. Once he got that thing to rocking and rolling, he'd stand back there, making soothing noises, and almost anyone would break down and give him all they'd ever known. After that, they'd lie back and believe anything he felt like telling them." He waved a hand back and forth as Don started to speak.

"Later, huh? We can discuss all the ins and outs some day when this is all over. Right now, let's be getting back to business." He smiled disarmingly and leaned back in his chair.

"Somehow, Stern's hand has got to be forced. He's off balance right now, and we want him further off. We want him to make a move he can't back out of. And you may be able to make him do just that."

"I might?"

"Yes. Suppose the hill tribes joined with the Waernu and demanded that a conclave consider Pete's claim to the throne. What then?"

"I guess there'd be a conclave."

"There might, at that. Now, let's go a little further. Suppose the Waernu claim were upheld and we got a new king — let's see, he'd drop a syllable — King Petonar. Where would our friend, Stern, end up?"

Don grinned wolfishly. "Khor Fortress. Even I can figure that much out."

Masterson stood up and paced around the office.

"So, if we can get Jasu and his son in motion and get them up in the Morek, something's bound to break. Right?" He stopped in front of Don.

"Oh, of course, Stern might call out the Royal Guard and scream rebellion. He'd probably do just that, if things went that far. He's getting in the propaganda groundwork for it now. But what he doesn't know is that he'd help us that way." He perched on Rayson's desk.

"You see, we've got some colonists that would yell at the top of their lungs for protection of their interests by the Federation. And then there would be a conclave — with plenty of supervision. Either way, he'd get right into checkmate." He clasped one knee in his hands and rocked back and forth.

"But there's one thing that stands in our way. Jasu Waern's scared to death. We've never quite dared explain this whole thing to him, and now no one can get near enough to talk to him. Harle was the clan head and the one with the nerve. He's gone, and Jasu's holed up. Won't let his son out of the house. Won't let anyone in. We can't move."

He got back to his feet and walked over to the window.

"Now, let's take some more suppositions. Suppose a flier went out of control and crashed in the middle of the Waern house. Or suppose some major criminal took refuge close to the place and decided to shoot it out with the Enforcement Corps. Seems to be a habit criminals have gotten into lately. And suppose a stray inductor beam just happened to graze the Waern living room.

"Then, who's checkmated?"

He looked down at his chair, then walked over and dropped into it.

"There's only one way to get Jasu in motion. You're it. The way you slammed Rayson back in his chair yesterday gave me an idea. You can get in there, and you'll have to move him — by force — compulsion — however you want to.

"Meantime, I'll get some things going. Your father can start the hill tribes getting together. He knows all the important head men. I'll give him a little push in that direction. Then, we'll get some more people to work."

Don looked at him for a moment. "Well, Dad told me I'd probably have to earn my keep. Anything else I ought to know?"

Jasu Waern looked up in annoyance, then got to his feet.

"Who are you?" he demanded. "How did you get in here?" He reached into a pocket.

Don Michaels spread his hands away from his body.

"Leave that weapon alone," he said sharply. "I came as a friend, and I'd hate to have someone shooting at me."

"But who are you?"

"I'm Donald Michaels. I want to talk to Pete ... Petoen, I should say."

"My son is seeing no one. There has been — —"

"I know," interrupted Don. "Trouble. Listen, I've had trouble myself in the past couple of days. It all started when I prevented a bunch of roughnecks from slapping Pete around." He frowned.

"Since then, things haven't been too pleasant." He held up a finger.

"I got accused of falsifying my report on the affair in the locker room. Pete didn't show up to testify, and everyone was looking at me." He extended a second finger.

"Pressure was put on me to sign a statement saying Pete used mental influence to make me put in a false statement. And I got into it with the school psychologist." A third finger snapped out.

"Next thing, I was being accused of accepting a money bribe from Pete. And I really got into it with the faculty advisor. That's not good." He dropped his hands to his sides.

"Right now, I'm not too popular at school. And I want to know what's going on. I want to know why Pete didn't show up to give me backing. I want to know what can be done to unscramble this mess."

Wearn shook his head slowly. "There are other schools — private schools," he said. "And we are still possessed of some — —"

"Careful, Mr. Waern." Don held up a warning hand. "I don't carry the sling, but I do come from the Morek. Don't say something that might be misinterpreted. I want to see things straightened out. I didn't come here to start a feud with you."

Jasu Waern shivered a little. "But you are galactic, are you not? Surely, you are no hillman."

"I was brought up among them. Now get Pete. I want to talk to both of you."

Waern looked unhappy. But he walked across the room and pulled at a cord.

A servant came to the door.

"Tell Master Petoen," ordered Waern, "that I would like to see him in here."

The man bowed and left. Waern turned back to Don.

"You see, Mr. Michaels," he said apologetically, "we are in difficult times here. My brother — —"

"I know." Don nodded. "Pete was upset the other evening. He told me a little. A little more than is made public."

Waern's eyebrows went up. "He said nothing about that."

Don waved negligently. "It did no harm. Maybe it was a good thing." He turned toward the door, waiting.

Pete came in, looking about the room. "You brought Don Michaels here, Father?"

Waern shook his head. "He came. He insisted on talking to you, Petoen. And I find he is very persuasive."

"Oh." Pete turned. "I'm sorry, Don. Father thought that I— —"

Don laughed shortly. "He was right—to some extent. But I'd like to talk to both of you about a few things."

He moved back, to perch on the edge of a heavily carved table.

"Let's look at it this way. I got into trouble over the affair. Not good, of course, but what happened to me is just one small incident. All over Oredan, good intentioned people have things happening to them. Sometimes, they're pretty serious things—like someone getting killed. And they usually can't figure out what hit them. These things happen pretty often. Why?"

Waern looked uncomfortable, but said nothing. Don looked at him curiously.

"Do you really think, Mr. Waern, that you can sit here in peace? That if you ignore this whole mess, it'll go away?"

Jasu Waern spread his hands. "What dare I do? My brother was trying to do something. He is gone."

"True. He tried to clean up a little here and fix a little there. And that only in one city. He didn't come boldly out and demand. He was playing on the edge of the board, not in the center. A king could do much more than that."

Waern looked at him, shaking his head.

"Yes, I know about the succession," Don told him. "And why shouldn't you demand? You could get the support of the hill tribes. All you need do is ask."

"I have thought of that. Perhaps we should have done that—once. But now? After my brother's death? And what could the hillmen do against the weapons of the plains?"

Don smiled at him. "Would the hillmen believe the stories about your brother in the face of your personal denial before their own council? Would they accept such a thing about any of the Waernu unless it were proven by strong evidence? Yours is one of the clans, even yet, you must remember. And how about the honor of the Waernu?"

Jasu's face was suddenly drawn. Don continued.

"And would the plainsmen dare use their weapons against a legitimate claimant? For that matter, what good would their weapons be against a Federation Strike Group, even if they did use them?"

"You seem so sure."

"Not just sure. Certain." Don glanced at his watch, then frowned.

"We've lost a lot of time." His voice sharpened.

"Come on," he snapped. "My sportster will carry three people. Let's get out of here while we can still make it." He made shooing motions.

Waern moved toward the door, then turned.

"To the Morek?"

"That's right. Up to the Morek. We're going to start a feud."

Andrew Masterson looked at the handset approvingly. Little Mike was getting the idea. He was still just as fast as he'd ever been. He made a little noise in his throat, then spoke.

"Well, if you have any questions, Mr. Michaels, feel free to call us here. Thank you, and good-by."

He dropped the handset to its cradle and leaned back again.

So that was set up. Little Mike would be on his way out to the hills by the time he'd completed this next call. And he'd have the clans ready for talks with the Waernu. Now, the next step would be to alert Jahns, down in the Resident Commissioner's office.

He looked at the surface of his desk, considering, then reached for the phone again. He'd have to be careful on this one.

The door opened and two men came through. One of them held out a card.

"Masterson?"

"That's right."

"Like to have you come with us. People investigating Rayson's accident have some questions they'd like to ask you."

"Oh?" Masterson's eyebrows went up. "I'm afraid I wouldn't be much help on that. I saw him go down, of course, but the view from this window isn't the best. I really — —"

The other shook his head. "Look, don't tell me about it. They just told us to come out and get you. Got a lot of experts down there. They'll ask the questions."

Masterson looked at the man appraisingly, then glanced at his partner, who stood by the door, leaning against the wall.

These two, he thought, would be no great problem. Nothing here but arms and legs. But— —

He smiled to himself.

It would be you or the whole tribe, he thought.

He might still be able to remain under cover, and he'd be a lot more effective that way.

So maybe they were a little suspicious. He glanced down at the desk. The little control box was safely destroyed and its operation had left no evidence. Even if they did suspect the cause of Rayson's crash, they couldn't prove a thing. No, his best bet was to go along with these two and hope the questioning would be short enough to allow him to brief Jahns with plenty of time to spare. He shrugged.

"Well," he said aloud, "I'll go with you, of course, though I don't see how I can be of any help. Terrible thing, losing Rayson that way."

"Yeah. Real bad." The other nodded curtly. "Come on. Let's go."

Daniel Stern looked angrily at his aide.

"Just who is responsible for this report?" he demanded.

The aide looked aside. "It came in from Riandar Headquarters, your honor," he said. "Colonel Konir signed it himself."

"I can read," snapped Stern. "But who's responsible? What idiot let this thing fall apart?" He shook the papers angrily.

"Look at this thing," he ordered. "Simple instructions were issued. With the organization they have up there, any fool could have carried them out. So long as they kept it simple, even an idiot could have eliminated that Waern nuisance. But no! Someone had to be subtle. Someone had to make a big project out of it. And, of course, something went wrong." He snorted angrily and slapped the papers down on his desk.

"Rayson was responsible in part, I suppose?"

The aide nodded unhappily and Stern let out an explosive breath.

"Your man! Well, at least, where he is, he can do no more harm. Tell me, are they going to get a confession out of that man, Masterson?"

"I doubt it, your honor. He claims to know nothing of the accident. And there isn't a scrap of evidence that— —"

"Evidence! There's very little doubt is there? With those notes of Rayson's? And who else could have caused the crash?"

"Well, there certainly is no other— —"

"Of course not. We know Masterson did it somehow. But why?"

The aide said nothing and Stern glared at him.

"Who is this Masterson?" he demanded. "Have you checked back on him?"

"He came here from Nogira," said the aide slowly, "seventeen years ago. He had some civil police experience there. We've checked that. He has a degree in criminalistic science. We checked that, too. Not a suspicious move since he came here. He was in the Civil Branch for a few years, then was assigned to instructional duty. He's got a perfectly clean record."

Stern shook his head slowly, then looked down at the desk again.

"Just that little," he growled. "He could have simply hated Rayson for some private reason. He could have seen him as an obstacle. We could care less about that." He tapped at a paper.

"Or, he could be working with the Waernu. And that's probable. He could even be an undercover agent for the Federation, though that seems a little improbable. He's been here too long. Hah! He could be almost anything except what Rayson thought." He looked up.

"Well, don't let him go. Keep him out of circulation. In fact, you better have him put in tight confinement. We'll look into him more closely later. Right now, I want to know what became of that Waern boy."

The aide pointed at the papers on the desk. "The boy and his father are reported to have left their residence, your honor. It is thought they went with that same Donald Michaels who interfered with the original plan."

Stern nodded. "The boy Rayson had right in his hands, and then let go. Yes." He looked around the room, then got to his feet.

"Tell me, has any progress been made on locating the Waern 'Book of Ancestors'?"

"No, your honor. Records has located and destroyed the last of the evidence here in Oreladar. But the Waern copy has not yet been located."

Stern nodded. "Find out who is responsible for the long delay in discovering the Waern claim, Lander. That is inexcusable." He frowned.

"Now, to the Waernu. Did anyone see them leave their home?"

The aide shook his head. "Observers say Michaels' flier landed in the Waern courtyard. A few minutes later, it took off and headed toward the mountains. The observers were unable to determine how many people were in the flier when it departed. It left too abruptly and traveled too fast. They determined its direction, but were unable to follow it."

"Valuable men! I think we should take careful note of all those people up at Riandar. Possibly they should be reassigned to duties more suited to their abilities. Tell me, did anyone have the elementary intelligence to have this flier tracked?"

"They tried, your honor. But it disappeared in the canyons, flying very low. Search fliers have been operating for several hours, but no trace of it has been found."

Stern nodded. "Well, we won't discuss it any further," he decided. "You know my feelings on the Riandar people. I should say it would be safe to assume the Waernu are holed up in Michaels' home. Get the exact location of that place. Then set up an Enforcement Corps operation." He frowned.

"Get some men out to make sure those people don't go into the hill country before we can take care of them. You can use the search planes for that. Then attend to your advance publicity and set up elimination. You'll give that personal supervision, all the way through. Clear?"

The aide nodded.

"Very well. See that you make it simple. I'm not going to tell you how to handle this in detail, but I expect to watch a broadcast showing their removal within the next three days. Get started."

"Yes, your honor." The aide backed out of the room.

Stern watched the door close behind the man, then faced around as a dry voice sounded behind him.

"Real nice, Danny," it said. "You went through it without a stumble. Even came up with something of your own. You're learning, Kid."

Stern glared at the scrawny man.

"I thought you picked those people up at Riandar. I thought you said they knew how to do things."

The other shrugged and spread his hands. "Well, Danny," he said, "you know how it is. Once in a while, we underestimate the opposition, and they slip one over." He leaned back in his chair, staring at Stern.

"But maybe this way, it's even better," he added. "We get a few in the net we didn't even suspect existed, you see?" He paused.

"I think you should have a talk with this Masterson yourself," he went on. "Maybe you should tell him to give us some of this information he has, eh?"

Stern looked at him in annoyance. "I expect you and the rest of the people around here to do some work, Gorham. After all, I'm the regent. Do I have to do everything?"

Gorham got to his feet and brushed some of the dust from his trousers.

"I tell you, Danny," he said seriously, "some of these little things, you have to be doing. Some of these things, only your talent will take care of, no?" He held up one hand, waggling a finger in the air.

Stern glared at him.

"Gorham," he snapped, "I think I'll have to remind you of your place." He tapped himself on the chest.

"I'm the regent, remember? I'm the kingpin here. You're just a senior executive secretary. You wanted it that way, and that's the way it is. But I expect you to start doing some work. I don't care how you get information out of that man, Masterson, but I expect you to get it. I certainly don't intend to do your work for you. Now get at it!"

Gorham considered him for a moment, then walked slowly across the room till he stood before Stern's desk.

"Now, Danny-boy," he said softly, "don't you go trying that funny stuff on old Jake. It don't work so good, remember? Nobody ever tells old Jake he should do things. Nobody!"

He planted his left hand on the desk before Stern and leaned over a little.

"We got an agreement, you and I, remember? I do the thinking. Me — old Jake Gorham — I'm the brain. You got this talent, see. You tell people they should go do something, they go do it. But not old Jake. No, no. With him, it don't work so good. Everybody else, maybe, but not old Jake." He waved his head to and fro, keeping watchful eyes on Stern.

The younger man slammed his hands to his desk, pushing himself back.

"You listen to me, old man," he snapped. "We had an agreement — once. And you've been using it to ride my back ever since. It's come to an end. Right now." He got to his feet, his deepset eyes seeming to flame.

"From now on, I'm the top man, do you understand?" His lip curled.

"I'm the regent. I'm the law. I tell these people what to do, and they do it. And I can tell them to take you out and shoot you. Don't forget that." His hand started toward a button on his desk.

Jake Gorham's hand blurred into motion and a small weapon was suddenly in it. He pointed it at Stern.

"Sit down, Danny-boy," he ordered menacingly. "Sit down. And listen. Listen real good." He spread his legs a little.

"Like I said, I'm the brains here. I do the thinking. Remember back in Tonar City? Remember what happened, you tried once to run things for yourself? Remember who came along and pulled you out just in time?" He laughed shortly.

"Yeah, you need old Jake. You gotta have him. You think you just tell these people—they should do anything you want. Oh sure. That lasts for a while, maybe, but they get tired. Just like on Konelree, remember? And what do you do when a whole mob moves in on you? Eh? What do you do? You ain't got the moxie to handle no mobs, remember?

"But old Jake, he thinks of things, and we both get along real good. Yeah, Danny-boy, you need old Jake." He glanced down at his weapon, then waved it from side to side.

"But you know something else? Old Jake, he don't need you so much. Oh, sure, it's nice here. I like it real good. But I got along real nice for a long time before I picked you up, you see what I mean. You didn't do no good at all. Talent, you got. But brains? No, them they didn't give you. And they didn't give you much guts, either, Danny-boy. Them, I got.

"And you know something else, Danny-boy? I got all kinds evidence. You done some pretty bad things here, remember?" He smiled, exposing yellow teeth.

"Real bad things, they wouldn't like them at all. And I can prove all them things. Me, I ain't got no responsibility. I'm just a poor, little old guy you keep around for laughs, remember?" He chuckled.

"You tell them to take me out and shoot me? I should laugh. You reach for that button. Go ahead. Stick your finger out. Then this thing here, it sings you a little song. And I go get some papers I got somewhere around here. And I go get some recordings. And maybe a few pictures. And then Old Jake's a public hero. And he takes a lot of money and goes away from here, he should spend his old age some place where he likes it better." He waved the weapon again.

"Still want to play?"

Stern's face was bloodless. He dropped into his chair, then put his head in his hands.

"I'm sorry, Jake," he said. "Sorry. I guess I'm just a little tired right now. Forget it, will you?"

"Sure, Danny-boy. Sure. We forget all about it. Now suppose we quit for the night, eh? Then in the morning, we get this Masterson fellow in here.

And you find out from him just who he is and why he comes here. And you can let him tell us what he's been doing and who he's been working with, eh?" Gorham smiled and stuck the weapon back in his sleeve.

"We ain't doing so bad," he went on. "We ain't doing bad at all." He reached out to stir the papers on Stern's desk with a forefinger.

"These people up at Riandar, they don't do so good maybe on that Waern kid. But they don't do so bad all the time. They get this Masterson, see? Right away, they're on him, soon as this guy Rayson gets himself killed off."

Stern nodded. "Yes," he admitted, "at least, they did have the sense to pick up Masterson—after he'd done plenty of damage. They were pretty slow. And they missed the Michaels boy entirely. So now, the Waern boy is out of easy reach." He frowned.

"We had things set up for an elimination on him, you know."

Gorham wagged his head. "Makes very little. Him, we can get. Him, they take care of in a couple days. Same operation, they should just move it a few miles, eh? Your boy with all them buttons, he takes care of that, see?" He grinned.

"And that takes care of this Michaels kid, too." Again, he poked at the papers.

"And here, we got another report. This young Michaels' father, he talks to this guy Masterson on the phone. You see that? And right away, he heads for the mountains. Maybe he wants to talk to the hill people, eh?" His grin became wider.

"But somebody at Riandar, he gets a rush of brains to the head, see? And the border patrol, they challenge this old guy, you get it? Just a routine check, see, but the old guy, he don't get the word so quick.

"So they don't take no chances up there. They knock him down in some canyon up there." He shrugged.

"So all this leaves this Masterson, you could talk to him, maybe he sings us some nice music." He turned away.

"I stay around, back at my desk. Maybe I should think of a question or two while we talk, the three of us, eh?"

The royal gold and blue receded from the screen and Merle Boyce's face looked out at his audience.

"This," he said shortly, "is the second day of the hunt for the Wells gang." He came out from behind his desk, his piercing eyes intent.

"For the past full day, this group of robbers have made their way toward the west. It is thought they hope to join rebellious hill tribes somewhere in the Morek region." He paused.

"Late yesterday afternoon," he continued, "these four men burned their way through a road block near Riandar. And despite reinforced blocks and stringent sky checks, they are still at large. All subjects of the realm are urgently requested to notify the authorities of any suspicious strangers."

He faded from the screen, to be replaced by the figures of four men.

"In co-operation with the Enforcement Corps," his voice continued, "we are showing pictures of the fugitives. We see here, Howard Wells, Merla Koer, Dowla Wodl, and Jake Milton." The voice stopped for a moment, then continued.

"These men are regarded as extremely dangerous. Subjects are urged to make no effort to approach them personally. Notify the authorities immediately if they are seen."

Don reached to the switch and snapped the receiver off.

"I don't like it," he said slowly. "I don't like any part of it."

"Think we might have visitors?" Pete looked at him thoughtfully.

Don nodded. "It could be just a build-up," he said. "Did you get that thrust about the tribes?"

Jasu Waern cleared his throat. "You mean those four are perhaps— —"

"I doubt if those four ever lived," Don told him. "At least not with those names. If we have visitors, they'll be more official—and a lot more dangerous." He paused.

"Wish Dad had come back. I'd like to get you off to the hills. Not so comfortable, perhaps, but it would be safer." He looked at the ceiling.

"Of course, with all those fliers chasing around right now," he added, "it might be complicated."

Pete looked at him curiously. "One thing I can't figure, Don," he remarked. "Why didn't you head right on into the hills from Riandar?"

Don spread his hands. "Intended to, hang it," he said. "They loused me up. Remember the dipsy-doodle I turned in that box canyon?"

"Think I'd forget?" Pete grinned. "Nearly got a busted head out of that one."

"Yeah. Well, I'd planned to jump the ridge and go on over to a clan village I know. We nearly caught it right there."

"We did?"

"Uh, huh. Some border patrol ship had a ripper. Lucky he got over-anxious. He cut loose out of effective range and shook us up. That gave me the news and I ducked for cover and streaked for home before he could get to us for a better shot."

"And now, you think perhaps they are trying to hunt us down as they did my brother?" Jasu Waern shook his head. "But this—it would be impossible to represent us as...."

Don tilted his head. "Nothing impossible about it—if they know where we are." He looked around the room.

"And it looks as though they do. Someone probably spotted my flier when I landed in your courtyard."

Pete looked at him unhappily. "Maybe we moved right into his hands. Maybe we're better targets here than we were in the city."

Don moved his head from side to side decisively. "Never happen. This mythical Wells gang could have been holed up in the city, too, you know. And there, you'd have no warning. You'd have no defense and nowhere to go. This isn't some little summer cottage, you know. We can give them a bad time."

Jasu Waern shook his head sadly. "Yes," he admitted, "we can, as you say, give them a bad time. But a flash or two from one of their inductors will destroy this house just as surely as it did my brother's cottage."

"Maybe." Don smiled. "I've got some ideas on that, too. But there's more to this house than you see from outside. This place was built during the border wars, you know. We've got a place to duck to."

Pete stood up. "What's that?"

"There's a basement under this house. Shelters down there. Even total inductor destruction of the house wouldn't hurt anyone down there." Don pointed with a thumb.

"Got entry locks right out in the court."

"But their clean-up crews. Where would you hide from them?"

Don shook his head, smiling. "They won't do too much searching," he said calmly. "If they actually do attack this place, they'll get some genuine resistance. And there'll be a Federation patrol out here right after the shooting, to investigate the destruction of a Galactic Citizen's property."

His smile broadened. "At least, that'll be a good excuse. You see, Mr. Masterson's alerted people at the Commissioner's office. They know who's here—or will, when the shooting starts."

"But with this build-up, it will seem like an ordinary hunt for a criminal gang." Pete shook his head doubtfully.

"No, I don't think so." Don walked over to the heavy door leading to the range.

"Better get some of the weapons up here now, though. We'll have to give them a little show."

Pete looked at him curiously.

"Why bother?" he asked. "Why can't we just duck into the shelter and let 'em blast? Then we could wait for the patrol."

Don shook his head.

"The type of resistance offered will be a tip-off to the Guard," he said. "I'm going to use an unusual type of weapon. Besides, Stern's people have detectors. Remember those? There's got to be life force in detector range, or they'll assume we've either deserted the place or found refuge below ground. Then they would come in for sure. And they'd really search the place." He smiled grimly.

"I'd rather take my chances on getting shelter from a blast after they commit themselves than take on a batch of those monkeys in a hand-to-hand down in the basement." His smile faded.

"It'll be touch and go, at that. The force of an inductor blast is nothing to joke about. We can roll into the ledges and hope, but we still might get singed a little." He sighed and spread his hands.

"Well, I asked for work. Guess I've got it. Sorry you may get scorched around the edges, but — —"

Pete looked at the heavy wall on the other side of the outer court.

"At least, we've got a better chance than Uncle Harle had. They probably tied him up. And no matter — —" He shrugged.

"All right, Don, let's get those weapons."

"Well, here they come." Don Michaels looked out of a weapons embrasure.

From the port, the advancing men were far more visible than they intended to be. One after another, they crawled and dashed through the grass, their weapons held before them. They concealed themselves from the house as best they could behind hummocks and clumps of grass. Then, weapons probing toward the house, they waited.

A couple of hundred meters from the house, a weapons carrier purred into position, wheeled to face the house, and stopped, the muted roar of its motor dying to a faint rumble.

Closer to the house, there was a hollow in the earth, a scar from some long-forgotten skirmish. Over the years, rain and wind had worked on it, softening its once harsh outlines. Grass had grown in, to further mask the crater, till now it was a mere smooth depression in the ground. From the edge of this depression, rose the slender rod of a speaker, a small, directional loud-speaker blossoming from it.

Michaels grinned and turned aside for an instant.

"Just like the big broadcasts, Pete," he remarked. "Feel important? You're going to have a big audience."

"Kind of like it better if I were making a personal appearance. Be a lot nicer if I could talk to them—and they could see my face."

"They can't let you do that," Don grinned. "You don't look enough like any of those guys they're supposed to be hunting. Spoil the whole effect that way."

Pete looked at him thoughtfully.

"You know, they always tell people to throw their weapons out and come out with their hands in the air. What would happen if someone took 'em up on it—like the wrong someone—like me, for instance?"

"Good question," Don told him. "Saw a guy come out in one broadcast. Someone vaporized him. No way of telling which direction the spray came from, of course. No tracer on the beam." He shrugged.

"Somehow, I don't think it would lead to a long and happy life."

"No." Pete nodded. "I didn't suppose it would." He looked at the long target rifle in Don's hands.

"You could have gotten several of them with that, while they were getting into position, couldn't you?"

"Suppose so," Don nodded. "But I'm saving it for a while. Got an idea, but it's a one-shot and I'll have to wait before I try it." He paused as a head appeared close to the base of the loud-speaker stand.

"Well, the show's about to start," he added quietly. "Here's the man with the serenade."

The speaker disintegrated in blazing fury and Pete turned away from the glare, to look back at the house.

"Took your father years to get this place built the way he wanted it," he remarked. "Shame you're going to have to lose it this way." He glanced over at his companion.

Don was stretched out in the prone position, his sling tight on his arm, the rifle extended.

"Yeah," he said. "But maybe we won't lose it—not just yet."

He rolled, forcing his elbow further under the rifle.

"Look, Pete, I think I'll wait till these guys are ready for the last act, but you better go ahead and take cover. They've committed themselves now. I'll duck later, if I have to, but I've got an idea that just might work out."

He laid his cheek against the stock, concentrating on his sights. The barrel moved up and down with his breathing, then stopped.

Pete examined him curiously, then looked out of his port.

The projector barrel was moving, to center its lens on target. As Pete watched, the lens barrel swung till he could see the glint of light on the outer focusing circles. As the rack with its charges started to face him, he moved back, preparing to roll into the narrow slit beneath the wall.

Now, the lens was pointing directly toward him, its iris beginning to widen. He slid off the ledge.

There was a sudden, snapping explosion near him. He looked up, to see the lens system disintegrate. The projector suddenly became a blue glare.

Pete watched as the tiny figures of the crew members flew back from their fiercely glowing weapon.

Abruptly, he realized he was in an exposed position. He ducked sideways, away from the opening, and covered his face.

There was a rumbling multiple explosion. Blinding light reflected from the walls of the house. A few tiles crashed to the court. Pete caught his breath again and risked an upward glance.

A tall pillar of flame had grown from the field outside. For long moments, it stood motionless, searching for a limit to the sky. Then it darkened. Smoke drifted toward the ranch house and bits of wreckage rained down upon house and field alike. Little puffs of smoke appeared in the sky, close by the still rising cloud.

"Pinwheel," said Don calmly. "That's one Dad couldn't beat if he tried. Wish he'd been around to see it." Suddenly, his forced calm deserted him.

"Oh, boy," he yelled happily. "Like shooting snakes in a pit." He shoved his rifle back through the port.

"Try to wreck our house, will you, you bums!"

A figure wobbled up from the field, weapon weaving unsteadily toward the wall. The rifle snapped viciously and the figure melted back into the ground.

There was another motion and a sudden spurt of dust followed immediately after the sound of a shot. The motion ceased.

The sound of the click of the rifle action was loud against the silence of the scene.

No more figures moved. Bright flames were growing — working toward one another, to form a widening lake of flame in the grass. Don sighed and started pulling the sling from his arm. Pete stood up, looking at him.

"I'm a little confused," he said slowly. "I thought that weapon of yours merely threw a solid missile. The way you described it, I thought it was just … well, something like a long-range throwing sling."

He looked out the port again, then pointed.

"But that weapons carrier was shielded. I didn't think you could touch one of those with anything but another inductor."

Don leaned the rifle against the wall.

"That's the way they figured it, too," he remarked. "But they forgot something.

"You see, rifles have been obsolete for so long everybody's forgotten their capabilities. Everybody, that is, except a few crazy hobbyists. And no one ever thinks in terms of long-range missile throwers."

"So?"

"So, I've been watching these clay pigeon shoots of theirs for a long time. They've had a lot of them on broadcasts, you know. And I noticed they always operate the same way. Actually … well, you saw them. They're not too careful." He smiled.

"Remember you remarked that I could have potted a few of them while they were getting into position? Only reason I didn't was that I didn't want to give them a warning." He shoved his hands in his pockets.

"You see, they know they're going to use that projector. The rigged speaker just makes it look good — as though the blast were necessary and unavoidable. That way, the public is convinced that the whole affair is a heroic battle against evil. See what I mean?

"So, they have everything all set up. Safeties are off. Activators are hot. Everything's lined up so they can look sharp. Snappy operation."

He shook his head with a smile. "But actually, they're a little overconfident. Their field screen will stop any heat ray. No khroal charge can get through—it'd get damped. The screen will ground out a Nerne-Herzfeld couple, and no bunch of fugitives is going to be lugging an inductor around with them. So there can't be any counter-battery fire. Result? The projector crew feels perfectly safe."

His smile widened. "But that isn't enough. They want to be comfortable, too. It's hot inside a deflector screen and they'd get their uniforms all sweaty and out of press. Besides, the screen draws a lot of power and they'd have to rev up their motor. The noise would make it rough for the sound crew. Catch?"

Pete moved his head. "I begin to get the idea," he said. "The inductors are real touchy when they're armed. They can arc over and flare back in a real hurry if things get in their fields. That's why the safety lens—and the iris."

"Sure." Don nodded. "Sure it is. And it keeps the beam tube nice and unobstructed. Dry, too. As I said, they're pretty safe. Just like pigeon hunters." He looked out at the field.

"Sort of funny how things can add up," he added. "Here's a guy who makes all sorts of plans. He's got everything figured out and tied up with a ribbon. He's got the whole Galactic Federation standing around, just watching. Not a thing they can do to him legally. And he's got all Oredan in his pocket—all but one family and a few odd yokels he doesn't even worry about. So he's about to fix the family.

"Then someone else starts planning. And some little guy goes and slips a little chunk of fast moving lead down a lens barrel that nobody even thought of protecting. And everything goes wrong. All kinds of things happen. Like investigating patrols ordered in by the Stellar Guard. And conclaves." He grinned and looked at the sky to the west.

"So," he added, "a few little things add up. One family. One little piece of lead. One house that didn't get blown up. One flight of— —" He let his voice trail off and looked at his watch.

"Wonder where those patrol ships are. They should be in plain sight by this time, diving down the eastern slope."

He narrowed his eyes, searching the empty western sky.

Pete looked around the courtyard. Broken tiles littered the ground. Here and there, lay bricks and bits of mortar. Some freak of backblast had torn a shutter off the house and it lay brokenly a few feet from him. He looked back toward the house.

One corner of the roof had been shattered and he could see broken roof beams. A cornice from the wall had crashed into the house front and bits of it lay strewn through a gaping hole in the living room wall. Stucco littered the narrow border of shrubbery around the house, whitening the green of the leaves.

And a twisted bit of metal caught his attention. Obviously, it was part of a flier. He shook his head and looked at the sky over the western mountains.

"Quite a blast," he said. "Look, Don, are you sure anything's coming to back us up? A couple more of these and we'll be standing in an open field."

Michaels reached up to stroke his face. "Right now, I'm not too sure about anything," he admitted. "Except that next time they try to comb us over, they'll take a few less chances." He frowned.

"Mr. Masterson was pretty certain about things, but— —"

He spun around and walked toward the flier port.

"You know, I think we'd better play it safe," he went on. "Right now, we've got clear air. That explosion put everything around here on the ground, but hard. But that won't last. Stern's people will be flocking around here in a few minutes to see what went on. We better not be around when they arrive. Go get your father."

He pulled the flier door open.

"I'll have this thing warmed and ready to flit by the time you get back up here. Make it fast, will you?"

Pete had already dived down an escape slot. As Don started through his pre-flight routine, he reappeared. Jasu Waern followed him.

"What happened?" The older man looked around the littered courtyard, then at the flier which Don had pushed out of its cover. His eyes widened.

"But I thought they would use an inductor."

"They tried," Don told him. "Come on. Get in." He looked anxiously at his instrument panel.

"Little risky," he muttered, "taking off so fast. Synchs and generators haven't had time to stabilize. But it beats letting them get in range for some more target practice."

He eased a lever toward him and watched the pointers on a dial as the flier lifted. The red needle started to oscillate and he reached quickly to adjust a knob. The oscillation stopped. He looked overside.

"Hm-m-m," he said, "so far, so good. Well, let's have at it."

He reached out and pulled a handle toward him, watching the needles. They remained steady and he nodded and pulled another control toward him, then gripped the control wheel.

The flier leaped into the air and surged toward the mountains.

Don sighed and made a minute adjustment on the synchro knob.

"Well, we haven't flipped yet," he said. "We'll stay on deck all the way. Not such a good target that way. Take a look back there, Pete. See anything in the air to the east?"

"Yeah." Pete had been looking back. "There's plenty back there. And they're in a hurry."

Don jerked his head around, then glanced at the mountains before them.

"So are we. They built this thing to win races, not lose them. Hope they knew what they were doing." He pulled a panel lever all the way back and the flier surged forward, pressing them back into their seats.

"Hang on," he said. "Some of these corners are going to be tight."

The ship swung into a narrow valley between two hills, bucking and twisting as Don worked the control back and forth. As a high cliff loomed up in front of them, he pulled the flier up, then around in a screaming turn. A second later, they almost touched the tips of trees as they swung around the shoulder of a steep hill. The flier dropped abruptly, seeking the floor of a gorge, then swung violently as it followed a swift flowing stream.

Don guided it into a side gorge, then suddenly pulled up, to jump through a notch in the surrounding hills. For an instant, the flier paused, hovering in the air over a deep, wide valley, then it dropped like a stooping falcon, sweeping sideways at the end of its drop, to come to rest under an overhanging rock formation. The pilot snapped off switches and leaned back.

"We've got a small-sized walk ahead of us," he said, "but it's through some pretty dense growth and we'll be invisible from the air." He grinned.

"The way I dove into that first canyon, anyone with detectors on me would assume I was heading for the Doer—if he knew the country fairly well. Hope that's the way they know it—just about that well."

He climbed out of the ship, holding the door open.

"Come on, Pete," he ordered, "give me a hand and we'll shove this thing back in the cave so it won't be too easy to spot."

Jasu Waern climbed out after his son.

"I shall help, too," he said resignedly. "Which of the clans do we join?"

Don put a shoulder against the side of the flier. "Kor-en," he said. "I know them pretty well. Matter of fact, the Korenthal wanted to adopt me at one time. Dad talked him out of it."

Waern nodded. "The Kor-en are known to us," he murmured. "Possibly — —" He added his weight to the pressure on the flier's side.

They pushed the machine far back into the cavern under the rock, then camouflaged its smooth lines with brush and rubble. Finally, they walked over the rough ground to a nearby thicket. Don paused, looking up. Then he pointed.

"There they are," he said, "in a search pattern. Guess they got a detector flash on us when we jumped the ridge." He shrugged. "Well, they've got a tough hunt now. We'll detour through that line of trees to keep out of the open."

He jerked his head, to point.

"There's a narrow break in the cliffs way over there. When we get through that, we'll come into Korelanni."

Halfway through the narrow crevice, Don stopped and turned aside, to enter a narrow alcove that had been carved out of the rock. Hanging inside was a long tube of wood. Don rubbed his hands vigorously on the moss which grew on the rocks, then stroked the tube.

A tone resonated from the chamber, growing louder as Don continued to stroke the tube. After a few seconds, an answering note of different pitch could be heard. Don nodded and stepped back into the path.

"It's all right," he said. "They'll meet us at the head of the path." He smiled.

"This way, we don't have someone dropping rocks on our heads."

Pete looked up at the towering cliffs which almost joined overhead.

"You mean they've got guards up there?"

"Always," Don told him. "Day and night. Right now, they're at peace with everybody, but they never let their guard down. We'll have a reception committee waiting for us." He started striding up the steep path.

At the head of the chasm, five men waited for them. In their hands, they held sticks about two feet long. At the end of each stick was a thong, with a flexible leather pad which could hold a fair sized stone. Don bowed in the direction of one of the group.

"I know you, Korendwar," he said.

The other bowed. "Michaels," he said. "I know you. And these?"

Don looked at him, his thoughts going into overdrive. The form of address was all wrong. Always before, he had been Donald, of the clan Michaels — they abbreviated it to Michaelsdon. But what had gone wrong now?

He tensed a little, then relaxed. At least, it was a friendly greeting. One does not "know" an enemy. He extended a hand toward Jasu Waern.

"I bring the Waerntal, Jasu. And his son, Waernpeto," he said.

The other nodded. "The men of Kor-en know the Waernu," he said noncommitally. "You want dealings with the Korental?"

Don nodded. "The Waerntal would discuss clan affairs with the Korental." he said. "I but serve as guide."

"It is well. You and this clansman may rest by the wells." Korendwar turned toward Jasu Waern, gesturing with his sling.

"I will conduct you to the Korental, your honor."

Pete leaned against a mossy bank and watched one of the village women as she raised a clay pot from a well.

"Tell me, Don, why did you push my father forward to consult with the Korental? Why didn't you go ahead and deal with him yourself? You said you knew him. Father doesn't."

"That's just the point," smiled Don. "I do know him. And I know his people, and his way of thinking." He waved a hand to indicate the entire collection of huts.

"These people are about as formal as you can get, when business is at hand. Did you notice the way I talked to Korendwar? Migosh, I've hunted with that guy, rolled around in the dirt with him when we were kids, know him about as well as you'd know a brother. But he was on guard. And, friend, you don't get informal with a clansman when he's on guard.

"This is just like a little nation, and the Korental is just as surely a ruler as any king of a huge country," he went on. "Even more so than most."

He fixed his eyes on the council hut, across the narrow end of the valley.

"Everyone in his clan is his child — symbolically, at least. He tells them what to do. He tells them what to plant and when — and how much. He tells them when to hunt, and where. Governs their lives down to some pretty fine points. I mean, he's as absolute as an absolute monarch can get.

"And if you want to get along with an absolute monarch, you treat him on his terms." He glanced at his companion.

"Oh, I don't mean this guy's a tyrant or despot," he added quickly. "These people are pretty proud. They wouldn't like a dictator — as such. But the Korental doesn't need force to govern his people. They do things his way because ... well, it's a matter of tradition. It's the only honorable way to do things. See what I mean?"

Pete shook his head doubtfully and Don frowned.

"Pete, your family was originally a mountain clan. I should think you'd know these customs better than I do."

Again, Pete shook his head. "I'm sorry," he said slowly, "but I don't. You see, my father and my uncle thought it would be better if I learned the customs and culture of your people and of the plainsmen. And they thought I should be familiar with the ways of the great cities."

He looked across the village at the great tree which shaded the council hut.

"You see," he continued, "my great uncle was king. And he had no children. He was getting old and it was agreed that if he died childless, his queen would then adopt me. And, of course, I would then be head of the Onaru, and king of Oredan." He smiled wanly.

"The agreement was not made public, of course. And the queen no longer lives. But signatures and agreement are recorded at Oreladar. And they appear in the Book of the Waernu, against my name. References in the Book of the Waernu are so arranged that I may be quickly removed, to be placed in an already prepared place in the Book of the Onaru, if the time should come. This and the fact that my mother was the daughter of a brother of the king, places me in the line of kings of Oredan." He shrugged.

"Especially since the king did, in fact, die childless.

"And this, in my father's eyes, meant that I should know of the plains, of the cities, and of the galactics, since there, he said, lies the power and wealth of the present day Oredan."

Don shrugged. "Wealth, maybe," he said quietly. "I'm not so sure about the power. The pressure of History is a very real thing, and I seem to remember noticing that every time some king has gotten into a jam with one of the other kingdoms or with his own nobles, he's had to raise the clans. And there have been times when that wasn't easy."

Pete nodded. "I know. The Onaru took the throne two hundred years ago, simply because the clans withheld support from the Chalenu — the Old Line."

"Yeah." Don picked idly at the bark of a tree. "And Stern's been trying to get the clans into hot water ever since he took over."

Pete looked at him for a moment, then looked about the village.

There was no orderly arrangement of houses, as could be found in town. Wherever someone had found a suitable spot, there he had embedded his poles. And there, he had erected walls, daubed them with clay from the nearby stream, and formed long, limber wands from the thickets into arched roofs, to be covered with long grass from the valley. There were isolated houses, and there were tight little groups of houses. Possibly, Pete thought, family groups.

No streets existed here, though generations of sandaled feet had beaten the ground into winding paths which led from houses to wells, and from wells to fields, and to the surrounding forest.

And there was no litter, as could be found in any city. No fallen twig or leaf was allowed to remain on the ground of the village. Grass and moss grew on unused ground and on hillsides, but before each hut, the growth gave way to the forecourt and the small garden.

Here and there, a bank by a path had been reinforced with clay cemented stones and over these grew the moss, to soften the hard outlines of the works of man. Here and there, a small, neat pile of material for building lay, to remind the onlooker that this was a still growing community. Pete leaned back.

"It's quite a bit different from the plains," he said, "and not as I thought it would be. I always thought the hillmen were wild and uncultured." He turned toward Don.

"But you still haven't really answered my question. Why is it my father has to talk to the Korental—alone?"

Don lifted a shoulder. "Simple enough," he said. "Your father is the head of your branch of the family right now. It's a pretty small clan branch—just the two of you, but he's the clan head—the Waerntal. Right?"

"I suppose so. Yes." Pete thought a moment. "Actually, I guess he's tal over more than just the two of us. We are the senior line of the family."

"Well, then. This is clan business. Your father wants to advance a member of his clan as a claimant for the throne of Oredan. He needs the support of other clans to do this. And this is important clan business. See?"

Pete rubbed at an ear. "I begin to get the idea, I guess, but it just doesn't make too much sense. He could have you speak for him. Or I could plead my own case, for that matter, couldn't I?"

"Makes all kinds of sense." Don shook his head. "Look, you can't talk to the Korental—not on even terms—not now. You're just a clansman. If he accepts you as king-to-be, then you'll be a sort of super clan head. Then you'll be able to discuss policy with him. But even then, only as an equal—never as a superior. He actually acknowledges no superior." He pointed to himself, pausing.

"Me? Good grief, I'm not even in this. I'm just a hired hand—not even a member of your clan. Before I could open my mouth, I'd have to be adopted into your clan and designated as a clan councilor. Even then, the tal would have to open the discussion.

"Oh, I can talk to the Korental as an individual who wants to get help from some of his people for a hunt, sure. And we can then arrange an exchange of goods. That's between him and me. But if I tried to talk to him on this affair, he'd throw me out of the village." He rubbed his cheek thoughtfully.

"And, come to think of it, if he thought you'd asked me to intervene, after he'd tossed me out, he'd probably feed you to the Choyneu. That, he'd regard as a selling of honor."

Pete looked at him quizzically. "I can just see him — or any other person, monarch or no — throwing you anywhere you didn't want to go. I'd say the throwing would be the other way."

Don laughed softly. "Oh, that." He shook his head. "Well, let's just say I don't think I'd care to try it out on a whole clan at once. Things might get a little complicated."

A short, heavily muscled man came out of the council hut. In his hands, he held his slender sling-stick. He paused as he got to the door, then shook out the thong. For a moment, he stood, glancing across the end of the valley, then he wound the thong about the stick, securing it at the end with a half-hitch.

Again, he looked in the direction of Don and Pete. Then he held up the stick and beckoned to them.

Don pushed himself away from the bank.

"Well," he said, "here we go. They've come to some sort of a decision."

They walked through the door of the hut, stopping as they came inside. An old man sat on a hide-covered stool, facing the entrance. Near him stood Jasu Waern. The old man got to his feet.

"Waernpeto?" he asked.

Pete stepped forward and bowed. "I am Peto of the clan Waern," he said.

"It is good." The Korental nodded briefly, then looked at Don.

"And Michaels. I know you," he added.

Don looked at him curiously. There was that odd form of address again. Had he suddenly come to be regarded as clanless? What was this? He bowed.

"I know you, Korental," he said formally.

The old man before him nodded.

"We are not now sure how to address you," he explained. "Your father may yet be alive, so we cannot regard you as clan head. But as your father has not been found you may, therefore, be clan head in fact. The men of clan Mal-ka have joined us in searching the gorge of the Gharu, where his flier was shot down. Thus far, nothing has been found. It is a long gorge, and deep."

"Dad?" Don blinked. "Shot down?"

The Korental nodded. "Two days since," he said. "A flier of the Royal Guard fired upon him and his flier weaved and dropped into the gorge. No man saw its landing place." He paused thoughtfully.

"Nor were there flames."

Don glanced about the hut. It was the same place he had come to many times before, when he wanted to get beaters. It was familiar. And yet it was now a place of strangeness. Suddenly, he felt rootless—disassociated from people. He struggled to regain his poise and retain the formal manner expected of him. He managed a bow of acknowledgment.

"I thank the Korental for this information," he said. "I beg permission to await further word under his protection."

Somehow, he couldn't imagine anyone succeeding in shooting his father out of the sky. Kent Michaels had been one of the hottest fighter men in the guard. And even if he hadn't been able to get away from the guy, he'd have taken him down with him. How...? He jerked his attention to the Korental.

The old man had inclined his head. "My clan is yours during this time of trouble," he was saying. He looked toward Pete.

"And you are he who would be King of the Oredanu?"

Pete nodded. "I am."

"I see. Your father tells me of certain agreements made many years ago. He tells me of relationships, and of your possible adoption into another clan. These things are true?"

Again Pete nodded. "These things are true."

The old man considered him for a few seconds.

"Among the men of the hills," he said, "the simple word of a man may be accepted. For only a clanless one would think of speaking other than the truth. But I am told the men of the low countries have no such faith. They require writings, and the speech of many witnesses. This is also true?"

The question was obviously rhetorical. Pete smiled ruefully, but said nothing.

The Korental allowed his lips to curl in a half smile.

"These customs of the plainsmen are not unknown to me," he said. "Men of my clan have gone to the low country and have dealt with the men of the cities. Even now, members of the Kor-en live in the cities. But on the clan days, they return to their home, here in the hills." He looked down at the matting on the floor.

"Your father mentions a clan book," he continued. "Do you have this with you?"

Pete looked at him, then at his father. His expression was suddenly blank.

Jasu Waern stepped forward. "This book is in a safe place," he said, "in Riandar."

Don closed his eyes for an instant. "Oh, Brother," he told himself, "the lights just went out! I'll bet they're tearing that house up, stone by stone, about now."

The Korental nodded slowly. "How safe?"

"Why," Jasu was thoughtful. "Why, the hiding place is known only to me—and to my son." He bent his head, then looked up, smiling confidently. "No, it could never be discovered by an outsider."

"The book must be produced," the Korental told him. He resumed his seat on the stool and folded his hands over a short staff.

"We of the clans would be happy to support a legitimate claimant to the throne of Oredan. We are not happy with the rule of this outlander who has forced himself into power. But we also recognize the rules and the customs of the nobles of the land, who must have proof of everything before they will act. We are not strangers to the conclave, you must remember. And we are familiar with the power of the outlander." He looked at Don.

"Tell me," he said, "do you have an interest in this matter?"

Don nodded. "I am not of the clan Waern," he said carefully. "But my interests have become tied with theirs. Should the Waernu fail, my father's lands would be lost. And the climate of this land would become unhealthy for me—as well as for my father, if he still lives."

"Yes." The Korental regarded him. "I can understand that. We are not as uncivilized as many think us to be. We watched the broadcast of an attack upon your house." He tilted his head.

"Tell me," he added. "The broadcast ended rather suddenly. The announcer mentioned technical difficulties. Can you explain this?"

Don relaxed. The formal session was over for a while.

"I took a shot at them," he said, "with a Ghar rifle."

"Ha! They do have a weak spot, then. We'll discuss this later." The old man looked at Jasu Waern.

"Let us suppose that this young man should ask to be adopted into your clan. What would your answer be?"

Waern looked confused. "Why — — But he's been giving us — —"

The Korental chuckled. "I know. He has some of those characteristics attributed by legend to clan talu, and to them only." He bent his head for a moment.

"Suppose I put it this way. When the clans and tribes meet for full consideration of your request for support, you will need strong council. And the councilor who presents your cause must be a member of your clan, of course. He must speak for you, the head of the Waernu."

Waern looked at him. "I see," he said thoughtfully. "And here, we may find strong council." He looked across at Don.

"You would consider this?"

Don paused. This, he thought, was getting serious. It had been fine at first. He had just followed instructions from an experienced agent. And there had been quite a thrill at being in the middle of things. But somehow, everything was flying apart. All at once, he was on his own.

And now — well, clan councilors were pretty responsible individuals. They were supposed to be the experts on law and custom. They were supposed to put things together — and keep them that way. He could remember daydreams he'd had once, of helping run a country. Some of them had been pretty dramatic. But — well, it was beginning to look like real trouble. If things went wrong, a councilor could get his neck on a block for sure.

Then he smiled inwardly. So what of it? How could he get into any more trouble? He already had the entire Enforcement Corps screaming for his blood. He'd killed off a Royal Guard projector crew, an entire Enforcement crew, and a few odd news people. They didn't like him. But they wanted him. The only way out of this one would be straight ahead. He nodded.

"Of course," he said simply.

The Korental came to his feet and grabbed his staff. Beside his stool was a battered tone tube. He swung the staff at the dented wood and a deep tone followed the sharp crack.

He wheeled upon the man who came through the door.

"Tell the Korensahn to come up here," he ordered. "And have him bring five men with him. We have a clan adoption to witness."

Don flexed his back and hunched his shoulders a little to get the packboard more comfortably settled. The darn things were heavy. He looked at the others, who walked along the road. Hang it, they seemed to swing along under their loads as though they were just taking a short walk before breakfast. He poked at the hard ground with his stick.

How had he managed to haul himself into this one, anyway? Blasted thing had all seemed so logical, back there in Korelanni. He reviewed the steps.

First, it had been essential that the safety and contents of the Book of the Waernu be determined. Without it, Pete's claim would be so vague as to be untenable. Especially before a conclave with the regent in active opposition.

Second, the book would have to be placed in safekeeping where it could be immediately produced upon demand. He frowned. That was a tough one. So anyway — —

Then, there had come the question. Who was going to get this book and bring it back — or protect it? Pete was too valuable and too vulnerable. He was known, and if any of the police agencies got their hands on him ... well, that would be all. So Pete was out.

Jasu Waern? Don grinned to himself. "Skip it," he told himself. He poked at the ground again with the stick. It was getting hot. And he was thirsty.

"Hope that gunk they used to monkey up my complexion doesn't sweat out," he told himself. "That would do it for sure."

He glanced up at the sky. It was getting close to midday. Ahead, he could see a few men sitting at the side of the road, leaning back against their packs. He went forward a few more paces, then selected a comfortable looking bit of moss.

So what had happened? A little guy named Donald Michaels had been disguised as a clanless mat maker. He leaned back against the pack. And, brother, had they given him a stock of mats to sell. This clansman in Riandar would be busy for a month, just unloading all these things from his stock.

He thought of those daydreams he had once had. A king's councilor, he had imagined, was a highly important, greatly respected individual. He had dreamed of himself, dressed in the ornate formal robes he'd seen in pictures of the old nobility. He'd pictured himself exchanging urbane chatter with other beautifully turned out characters, who hung on his every word. He'd seen himself striding between low-bowing lines of assorted courtiers and soldiery, pausing now and then to tap at the pavement with his jeweled staff. He'd — — Hah!

He looked at the dusty trail. He'd been striding, all right, but the field reeds didn't look too much like bowing lines of — — Yeah, and his staff didn't have too many jewels, either. No pavement, even, and this fool pack didn't feel much like a finely tailored robe of office. He shrugged.

"This is no dream," he told himself. "You let one of Stern's people get suspicious, and you'll find out just how real things can get." He twisted around to get the package of food and the water bottle which dangled from the pack.

Distastefully, he looked at the little packet of powder which was in the food package. He glanced around quickly, then dumped the powder into his mouth, quickly gulping water to wash it down.

"Gaah!" he growled, "does it have to taste like the inside of an old shoe? Oh, well, it'll keep me nice and dark for the next thirty hours or so." He pulled a strip of dried meat from the package. Maybe this will help take the taste out.

He sighed and worked his jaws on the leatherlike substance. It started to soften a little.

Well, anyway, he knew how to get to the vault where the ancestral volumes of the Waernu were kept. And he knew just which volume to pick out. Only one small problem remained. How was he going to get into the house — and on into the little pond in the inner garden? He grinned as he thought of Pete's remark.

"It'll be simple for you," he had said enviously. "All you have to do is tell any guard you meet to stand aside and forget he ever saw you. Then you go on down to the vault. Wish I had that ability of yours."

"Sure," he told himself, "hang your clothes on yonder bush — and get right into the water. It's just a simple matter of diving down ten feet and pushing the right rock the right number of times — in the right directions. Nothing to it. And then you go through the pressure trap, and there you are. Simple!"

And who was going to guard the pond while he was down there? Suppose he broke surface right in front of a flock of trigger-happy Enforcers? He sighed.

"Oh, well," he told himself. "You asked for it. Now, you've got it. Have fun." He looked into the food package and selected a meal cake.

At last, he dusted his fingers and leaned back lazily against his pack, looking into the clear sky. For a few minutes, he simply relaxed, his eyes fixed on the infinite distance, his mind a near blank.

Other pack-laden men strode past him, intent on their destination. At last, a group swung by and the sound of their conversation brought Don out of his semitrance. Behind the group was another, who walked a little faster than the others, in an apparent effort to catch up. Don pushed himself up with the aid of his staff, drew a few deep breaths, and started pacing along behind him.

Ahead, the group went around a curve in the path. The man ahead of Don cut over into the grass, still intent on catching up with his companions, who were not more than a few meters ahead. Don watched him casually.

There was no use, he thought, in trying to keep up with this fellow or his companions. It was too hot. Besides, this was probably a clan group who would not welcome company — especially the company of one of no clan.

He started to slow down to a normal pace, then his attention was caught by movement by a rock just ahead of the other. A small, greenish-brown body was vaguely outlined in the long grass nearly in the man's path.

Don looked more closely. The animal was heavy-bodied, with rather short forelegs. Powerful hind legs were tucked under the body, twitching a little now. The forelegs pawed slightly at the grass and the flat, wide head probed out, extending toward the approaching man.

"Hey!" yelled Don. "Look out. Gersal!" He started forward in a half run, his staff poised for a blow.

The other jumped sideways but the furry body grazed his leg and spun, claws and teeth working furiously. The man looked down and screamed.

Don's staff came down in a chopping blow and the animal bounced out onto the open path. Its paws raised little spurts of dust as it spun about and prepared for another spring.

Again, Don's staff swung down. The gersal flopped about for an instant in the dust of the path, then faced toward him, an angry scream coming from its throat.

Again, it tried to get its balance for a spring, but one hind leg dragged limply. Again, the staff swung, tumbling the beast over in the dust.

There was a flurry of paws and the gersal struggled up to its haunches, then sat up, its brilliant red eyes fixed on Don. It stretched out short forelegs in seeming supplication, then batted futilely at the punching staff end.

Disregarding the pleading attitude of the beast, Don continued to punch at the squirming body till it was obvious that no vestige of life could remain. Then, he looked at the other man.

The fellow had managed to get to the center of the path before he had collapsed. He half sat, half lay against his pack, breathing raggedly. Sweat stood out on his forehead. He looked at Don vaguely, making an obvious effort to focus his eyes.

"Thanks ... Friend," he mumbled. "You tried — — Oooh!" He closed his eyes and stiffened, his legs stretching out and his back arching.

The men who walked ahead had been attracted by the commotion. They came back and one jerked off his pack and bent over the man in the path. He looked over at the dead animal, then glanced up at Don.

"How many times was he bitten?"

"I doubt if he got more than one," Don told him.

The other nodded and looked searchingly at the victim. Then, he reached into his clothing and removed a small packet. He opened it and pulled the protective cover off a syrette.

"There's a small chance, then," he remarked. He poked the needle of the syrette into the sufferer's forearm and squeezed the tube.

The stricken man moved convulsively and opened one eye. His companion nodded.

"You might make it, Delm," he said cautiously. "Only one bite, and we got to you soon." He nodded.

"If you can hang on for just five minutes, you'll walk the trail again." He looked up at Don.

"That was quick action," he said. "You may have saved our clan brother." He looked down at the torn place on the man's leg.

"A couple of more bites, and he'd surely be dead by now." He got to his feet.

"Whom do we have to thank?"

Don looked down at the path in apparent discomfort.

"I am Kalo," he said, "of the mountains."

The other's eyes clouded. "Oh," he said tonelessly. He looked down at his companion, then back at the dead animal.

"Well," he said slowly, "we are grateful, Clanless One. Go your way in peace. We will take care of our brother."

Don started to turn away. "I hope he — —"

The other nodded curtly. "The gersal's poison is strong," he said. "But soon we shall see. May your way be safe." He turned back to his patient.

Don turned away and went around the curve in the path. Well, maybe the Korental had been right, he thought. So long as they kept from bothering others, the clanless ones weren't molested. And they certainly didn't form any associations that might be embarrassing later on. He glanced back.

"Hope that guy lives through it," he told himself, "but I'm glad I don't have to put up with a three-day celebration. Haven't got the time."

In the distance, he could see the walls and towers of Riandar. The walk was nearly over now. He stepped his pace up a little, then slowed down again. There was no sense in coming through the gate all hot and sweaty, he reminded himself. It would be way out of character.

It was funny, Don thought, that he hadn't remembered this store when the Korental had described its location. Probably it was the use of the word "shop." This was a large department store. He'd done some shopping here at one time or another, himself. He started to go by the front, then a display in one of the windows attracted his attention. He paused.

Someone had designed a tasteful array of furniture, set up like a nobleman's bedroom suite. One could, without too much effort, imagine himself standing on the enclosed walkway of a palace, facing away from the inner garden. The furniture, he noted, was of excellent quality. In fact, when he started refinishing the ranch, maybe he'd come in here. He glanced at the display floor. The mats were similar in design to those in his pack.

Suddenly, he remembered his own present status and stepped back, away from the window. Simple mat makers don't concern themselves with examining displays that would cost more than they'd make in a lifetime. This window was strictly for people who could afford large platters of luxury. He turned away, looking for another, less elaborate entrance.

Down the street, at the corner of the building, he found an inconspicuous door. A brass plate indicated that this was the employees' entrance to the Blue Mountain Mercantile Company's offices. Another plate indicated that the delivery entrance was around the corner. Don shrugged and went into the door.

He found himself in a narrow hallway. Before him was a stairway, its lowest step blocked by a light chain. To his right, a man sat in a small cubby.

"You're in the wrong door," he said expressionlessly. "Deliveries are received around the corner."

"I know," Don told him. "I'm from the Kor-en. I'd like to see Korentona."

The man frowned fleetingly. "Tell you," he said casually, "maybe it would be better if you made your delivery right now. Then you can come back later on."

Don examined him for a moment. "You mean something is — —"

"That's right." The man nodded. "Go around to the receiving room. Drop your pack, and come back — say in about an hour." He glanced upward as footsteps sounded on the stairs.

"Oh, oh," he added softly. "Keep quiet and let me handle this."

A heavy-set man came down the stairs. He looked sharply at Don, taking in his appearance and the details of his pack.

"What's this, Mora?" he demanded.

The timekeeper shrugged casually. "Just some porter," he said negligently. "Can't read too well, I guess. Got in the wrong door. I was telling him where to drop his pack."

"Oh?" The other looked at Don more closely. "Looks like another load of those mats from the Morek. Look, Fellow, you wouldn't be from one of those clans, would you now?"

Don shook his head. "I am Kalo," he said, "of the mountains. I have no clan. I make mats. And twice a year I come here to Riandar to sell them."

"Been here before?"

"I have been in Riandar many times."

"That's not what I mean. Have you been here — to this store — before?"

Don shook his head. "Not to this store, no. But they told me the Blue Mountain was paying better than some others. I thought I'd try — —"

"Yeah," the other said coldly. "Sure. Now, suppose we take a little walk, you and I? Some people down the street would like to talk to you."

Don shook his head. "I merely came here to sell mats," he insisted. "I make good mats."

The heavy man frowned. "Maybe," he snapped. "We'll see about that after we've had a talk with you." He stepped closer. "If you're just a mat maker, nothing will happen to you. If you really have good mats, you might even get a nice price for some of your stuff. Come on."

He reached out to take Don's sleeve. Don stepped back, his face suddenly losing its vague, apologetic expression. His features sharpened, to become hard, uncompromising.

"Get over to that wall, Fellow," he ordered sharply. "Move!"

The man's hand dropped. For a moment, he stared slackly at Don.

"Come on!" Don's voice raised a little. "Get over to that wall. And then stand still." He started to shuck off the straps of his pack.

The man before him sobbed helplessly, then shuffled away. Don knelt down and stripped the pack off. Then he stepped aside and raised a hand in a beckoning gesture.

"Now get over here," he snapped. "Pick up that pack and take it up to Mr. Tona's office. I'll follow you."

The man in the cubby rubbed his head for a moment, then picked up the phone. Don swung toward him. "Put that phone back," he ordered, "and come out of there. You're coming with us."

Korentona looked up as the small procession entered his office.

"What's happened now?"

Don nodded at him, then faced the man with the pack.

"Put that pack down," he commanded. "Now, stand over there." He pointed. "And be very quiet." He glanced at the doorman.

"You can stay where you are." He looked at Korentona.

"My apologies," he said, "for being so informal. But I come from the Kor-en, and I had a little trouble. There's a message for you in the pack. You know, of course, where to find it. Who are these two?"

Korentona looked worried. "This one," he pointed at the doorman, "is a trusted employee. He's been with me for years."

He paused, looking at the other man. "But this one, I have never trusted. I'm sure he reports to the police."

Don glanced at the doorman. "My apologies," he said. "You are free to go as you will." He looked closely at the other.

"Is this correct?" he demanded. "Are you a police agent?"

The man nodded. "That's right," he said reluctantly. "I'm supposed to watch this place and report on its visitors."

"Here," Don told him, "is one visitor you won't report." He stopped, considering, then impaled the man with a cold stare.

"Have you ever seen a man bitten by a gersal?"

The man shrugged. "Yeah. What about it?"

Don nodded. "You will remember that scene," he said. "Do you remember that man's struggles? Do you remember the animal, chewing at him, injecting its poison? Do you remember this man dropping, first to his knees, then to his back? Do you remember — —"

"Hey!" protested the other. His hands came up before his face.

"Put those hands down," snapped Don. "And listen closely. I want you to have full recall on this. You remember this man who was bitten, how he sobbed for breath—how his legs stretched out and his back arched, till the muscles tore from the bones with their effort. You remember all this?"

The man nodded wordlessly, his fascinated stare fixed on Don's face.

"Then I want you to fix this in your mind," Don told him. "Should you be so unwise as to attempt to mention any of these things that have happened since you came down those stairs—should you even allow your memory to dwell on these things for too long—these are the things that will happen to you.

"You will sink to your knees. Your muscles will be unable to support you, and you will fall to your back. You will find it impossible to breathe, for the muscles of your chest will distend the ribs. And in your struggles, you will break bones. And you will tear your body to bits. Do you understand this?"

The man sagged against the wall, panting. He managed a nod.

"Then forget about this afternoon," commanded Don. "Go about your business in normal fashion. And forget about this afternoon. Nothing happened that was worthy of note." He waved a hand in dismissal, then turned to Korentona.

"I don't want to go into a lot of detail," he said. "As I said, there's a detailed message in the pack. I'll wait for you to read it." He glanced down at his clothing.

"I'd like a place, though, where I can clean up. And I could use some other clothes, if you don't mind."

When he came back to the office, Korentona waved him to a chair.

"So," he said musingly, "they were right. You did go to the clans for aid." He smiled.

"The police have been keeping close watch on everyone in the city who might have even a remote connection with the hill clans. And they're really keeping an eye on the Waern home. You're going to have a nice time getting in there."

Don nodded. "I expected some trouble. Do you know whether they've done any searching?"

Korentona shrugged. "I don't run an investigative agency," he said with a smile, "so I don't know everything that's going on. But I've heard there've been lights on up there nearly every night. And they've had crowds of people around the place. Not so much activity the last couple of days, though. They're just watching."

"I see," Don nodded. "Wonder if they've found what they were looking for?"

The other shook his head, "Doubt it," he said. "If they had, they'd relax. Now that I know what it's all about, I can figure out what I've heard. They'll take off the watch as soon as they find that book, I think.

"Oh, of course, they still want you," he added. "And they'd like to get their hands on the Waernu. But they wouldn't be frantic about it if they weren't worried about the outcome of a conclave."

"No," agreed Don. "I guess they wouldn't, at that."

He stretched. "Well, guess I'd better get on my way. I've got to get into that house somehow. Think I'll take a wander out there and see if I can get some ideas."

The merchant put up a detaining hand. "Take it slow," he advised. "You can't go up there tonight."

"Oh?"

"No. It wouldn't be wise at all. There are a bunch of young fellows that have been hanging around there lately. It isn't safe to walk around that neighborhood. They've beaten five or six people pretty badly. And they've killed a couple." Korentona paused.

"Funny," he added. "The police don't seem to be so upset about that."

"They wouldn't be," Don told him.

"So you think I'd better wait till morning?"

"It'll be a lot better. I can give you a place to stay tonight. And my house isn't too far from the Waern place, so you can get over there in a hurry if you want to." Korentona paused.

"Say, how about that fellow, Foree? Are you sure he'll keep quiet?"

Don smiled. "Pretty certain. Of course, I don't know whether an effort to talk would actually kill him. But he'd be pretty uncomfortable for a while. Might even come up with shock amnesia." The smile broadened.

"He may have already done enough careless thinking by this time to make him pretty sick." He regarded Korentona thoughtfully.

"You say there's a gang of young fellows hanging around the Waern neighborhood?"

The merchant nodded. "Quite a few of them, I think. People living around there don't spend any time on the street or in the park, you can be sure of that."

"I see." Don nodded slowly. "That way, it's a lot easier to watch the Waern place at night. Look, there must be quite a few hillmen in this city. I should think you'd know quite a number of them."

"Yes, I do, of course." Korentona smiled. "We don't exactly form a closed group, but ... well, I'll have to admit we do think a little differently from the plainsmen."

"I know." Don reached into his jacket and slowly withdrew a stick with a thong wrapped around it.

"Many of your friends carry these?"

The merchant laughed. "Certainly!" He produced a polished stick of his own.

"Can you imagine any clansman without this sling?"

Don looked at him speculatively. "I wonder," he said casually, "what would happen if these young toughs found themselves being hunted down by ... say ten or fifteen blood hungry clansmen. Might worry them a little, wouldn't you think?"

Korentona shook his head doubtfully. "You know what the situation is here in Riandar," he remarked. "The police don't worry too much about these robberies and beatings. But they'd be pretty perturbed if someone started hunting the hunters."

"That's what I mean." Don spread his hands. "Might even get the people watching the Waern place upset and nervous." He shrugged. "And who's to know what caused the uproar, or who's involved? After all, all the clansmen were at home. The watchers on their houses could testify to that."

Korentona looked at him curiously. "Interesting idea, at that, you know." He got to his feet. "Suppose we talk it over for a while."

Maurie VanSickle crouched behind a bush, watching the path. This, he thought, was getting old. It had been a lot of fun at first. Profitable, too. He thought with amusement of the old man who had scrambled about in the dirt that first night. Boy, what a beat jerk he'd been. And what a beautiful job Gerry had done on him. Clipped the stupid yokel so hard he didn't make a sound when he went down.

Then he and Walt had come in. Man, how the old guy had wriggled! He looked down the path.

Now, though? Phooey! Not a lousy person on the path all evening. He'd tried to tell Gerry they were on a loser. Park was all worked out for a few weeks. But the stubborn clown wouldn't listen. Kept insisting they try it a couple more nights. Maurie reached into his pocket.

"Better make a strike pretty soon," he muttered to himself. "The old cash bag's getting empty." He stretched, then tensed. There were footsteps on the path.

This one was his!

Silently, he gathered himself. He'd clip the guy from behind, then Gerry and Walt could come in from the other side and pin him down.

"Hope the jerk's got plenty of that stuff," he muttered.

The stroller came closer. Maurie appraised him as he walked. Oh, boy, another little, old guy. Clothes looked pretty good, too. Nice stack of cloth. Should be quite a rack of the purple in them.

Now the man was almost close enough. Maurie's eyes followed him as he approached, then passed. He launched himself in a crouching dash.

As he left the shelter of the bush, something bumped against his neck. He found himself whirling to the ground. Dimly, he saw his intended victim whirl around. He attempted to dodge the foot as it came down on his face, but it was like moving in a dream. Somehow, he was too slow.

For just an instant, he felt crushing pain, then the world dissolved into bright specks in a spreading blackness. One by one, the points of light winked out. And then, there was nothing.

As their intended victim whirled to crush Maurie, Gerry Kelton poked at his brother.

"Come on," he urged. "He can't take two of us. Let's go."

The two dashed out of their cover, then found themselves prostrate at the edge of the path.

Walt Kelton was flipped over and held in a vicelike grip, his head grinding into the path. Close by, he could see his brother. Two men held him down. As he watched, they seized Gerry's hands, twisting them so that his head flopped face up.

A third man leaned over, a long knife in his hand. Unbelievingly, Walt watched as the man thrust the knife into Gerry's throat. The boy's feet kicked convulsively a couple of times, then dropped. The toes sank, to point outward.

With calm precision, the killer turned his knife and forced it across the throat with the heel of his hand. Dark fluid welled out on the path, making a pool which flowed toward Walt.

Casually, the man pulled the slack of Gerry's shirt toward him and wiped the blade till it was gleaming again. Then he looked toward Walt. He got to his feet.

For an instant, the boy lay limp, paralyzed with terror. Then, he kicked and struggled madly. Unbelievingly, he felt the hands which restrained him loosen and he kicked and squirmed until he was free to scramble away.

He skittered on all fours till he reached the middle of the path.

Then he struggled to his feet.

And ran.

Don Michaels flipped on the light in the vault and looked around him. Yes, it was just as Jasu Waern had said it would be. He walked over to the closet at the side of the room and pulled out a towel. As he dried himself, he continued his examination of the room.

It had been easier to get in than he had hoped. When that screaming kid had come dashing along, it had been like a stick in an ant hill. Everyone around the house had been shaken up. Several men had gone streaking over to the park. The others had given the incident their full attention.

And all Don had needed do was walk up to the front door and go in.

"Guess they thought they had a full-scale revolution on their hands," he told himself. "Wonder how many Hunters the Moreku nailed." He grinned.

The men Korentona had talked to had jumped at the plan like starving gersals. Several of them had been victimized in the past. They really wanted blood. The others saw a good hunt in the offing. Every one of them knew someone who had been robbed. He'd turned something loose, all right.

"Hope they don't get too enthusiastic about it," he said. "Hate to have 'em make a habit of that sort of thing." He shrugged.

"Oh, well, let's see where that book is."

The sides of the room were lined with books. Over in a corner was a reading table with writing materials and a conveniently placed light. Don walked over to a glass-fronted bookcase and opened it, studying the titles of the volumes within. Finally, he selected a book and carried it over to the reading table.

He leafed through the volume, noting the careful engrossing. Then he paused as he came to the pages he was searching for. He examined the ornate script closely, then looked at the intricate stamp. It was the signature stamp of the old king. Beside it was his queen's less pretentious stamp. Don nodded in satisfaction.

Now, the only problem was to wrap the book safely in the waterproof tissue he'd brought with him, and get it out of the house. He stood, looking at the door.

It might not be too safe to leave the book with Korentona, as had been originally planned. With the clansmen under surveillance as they had been, and now, with this additional disturbance, there could be a disastrous slip. Don shook his head.

Somehow, the idea of carrying this document in a peddler's pack didn't make too much sense, either. Too many things could go wrong. He sat back in the chair and stuck his legs out.

"Well," he told himself, "I can't stay here for the rest of my life. I'll have to do something." He grinned ruefully.

"The best defense," he quoted, "is a determined and well-directed offense. So, if you don't know what to do, do anything. Then you'll find out what to do next."

He snapped the light out and opened the door. At the edge of the water lock, he breathed deeply a few times. Then he plunged in, closed the underwater door, and swam rapidly toward the surface of the garden pool.

He climbed out of the water, strode forward a few steps, then stopped in consternation. The place was suddenly flooded with light.

An oily voice sounded in his ears.

"Just stand still, young fella. That way, you don't get hurt. Not right away, anyhow."

Don turned. At the side of the garden, stood a scrawny old man, his seamed face wrinkled into a sardonic smile. In his hand, he held a small weapon.

Don recognized it—a khroal. The weapon could put out vibration which would tear any target to tiny, singing fragments in a few microseconds. It was a complete anomaly which had been in the possession of the Khlorisanu for measureless time. Its origin was mystery, its exact principle of operation a puzzle. But it was easy to duplicate, and it was one of the most deadly hand weapons known.

He held his hands out.

"Put that thing away," he snapped coldly. "Get it down—quick!"

The older man's smile broadened into happy amusement.

"Oh, funny stuff, eh?" he said joyfully. "I kinda hoped you'd be the one they'd send. Yeah, I kinda wanted to see you—what you look like, eh?" He waved the weapon.

"Just stand still, young fella, so old Jake can get a good look at you. Hey, you look like one of these here natives." The man bobbed his head.

"Woulda fooled me, you know?" He looked reproachful.

"Only, a smart young fella like you, you oughta know better than go and get that Foree so worried. You know, that fella, he comes in every night — got a lot of things he wants to talk about. Got theories. Got plans. Real eager fella. Only tonight, he ain't got nothing. Just grunts.

"Nothing goes on today, he says." Jake shook his head reproachfully.

"You know, that was careless. You shoulda let him talk anyhow a little, see. Something like that happens, old Jake, he gets ideas. So I come out here, to see who comes along." He looked at the package under Don's arm.

"That the book we're all looking for?" He jerked his head toward a door.

"Yeah, guess it is. Come on, young fella, that funny stuff, it don't work so good with old Jake, see? So let's you and me take a nice little ride. What ya say?"

The khroal remained steadily pointed at its target.

Don hesitated. This was about as far from good as it could get, he thought. Now who was this? Where did he fit into the situation?

"Who are you?" he demanded.

"Oh, I don't mind telling you that. Name's Jake. Jake Gorham. But come on. Let's get on our way. We got a nice, long ride, you and me, see?" Gorham waved his weapon again.

"Come on," he repeated. "Nice young fella like you, he don't wanna get all scattered around. Shame to mess up this nice pretty little garden, you know?"

Don hesitated. Of course, he might be able to dive into the pool again. But the khroal could kick out a cone several feet deep. There was no escape that way. No way out of the pool, anyway — except through this garden. He moved in the indicated direction.

Gorham herded him to the courtyard and closed the door. The house lights filtered through curtains, to show the outline of a flier in the middle of the court. Gorham urged him toward it.

"All right, young fella," he said, "just stand real quiet for a minute. I'll get this thing unlocked and start them synchronizer things." He reached toward the door, then paused.

"Yeah, I been kinda wondering about you," he added conversationally. "See, I got a smart young fella down there in Oreladar. He's got people pretty well trained down there by now. Chap named Stern. You hear of him, maybe?" He chuckled.

"Kinda set him up in business here a few years back, and he's doing pretty well. Old Jake just hasta hang around—kinda look after things now and then, this boy shouldn't get in too much trouble, see?" He cleared his throat.

"See, this Danny, he ain't got too much in the brains department. And he don't do so good when people get violent. Might say he sorta scares easy sometimes. Now you, I'd say you were a little different, see? Ya know, I just might be able to use a real smart young fella like you." He flipped the khroal up and down negligently.

"Now, don't go making up no mind yet. Like I say, we got time. We have a nice, long talk on the way to Oreladar. Maybe we work something out, eh? You know, old Jake, he ain't such a bad guy. You ask Danny. He'll tell you. We could get along real nice, the three of us." He paused, considering.

"Oh, maybe you don't like the idea at first," he added. "But we got all kinds ways to persuade people.

"Got a fella, name's Masterson, down there right now. Danny tries, but he can't do nothing with him. But he'll come around. You give us a few more days—a week, maybe, he's going to be a real reasonable fella." He pulled the flier door open.

"We're getting this country organized, see? One of these days, some fella's been smart and got in at the right time, he's going to be quite a guy. Have just about anything he wants, see?" He reached into the flier and snapped switches. A muted humming sounded through the courtyard.

"Tell you, though, Kid. Maybe old Jake's not real trusting like he oughta be. Not just yet a while. Suppose you just turn your back to me for a minute, eh?"

Don turned slowly, straining his ears.

He could hear the faint sibilance of Gorham's clothing as the man approached. Then the sound stopped. There was a slight grating noise.

Obviously, then, the man was lifting an arm and shifting his weight.

Don dropped suddenly to the ground, whirling as he went down. He seized Gorham's legs, lifted, then dashed the man's body to the ground. Swiftly following up, he seized the gun hand and twisted violently.

Jolted by the sudden fall, Gorham was quiet for a fraction of a second. Then he burst into explosive action, trying to tear himself free from Don's restraining grip. He twisted and tried to kick himself free, then groaned as the twisting pressure ripped at elbow and shoulder tendons. The khroal rattled on the stones.

Abruptly, Don jerked the tortured arm around and pinned it beneath a leg. He placed a hand on Gorham's throat and reached for the other arm.

"Aw," whispered Gorham agonizedly, "aw, take it easy, will you? I got the idea all right. So let me up, we do things your way, huh?" He looked anxiously at the face which stared down a few inches from his own.

Don saw the pleading expression on the man's face. For a heartbeat, he started to relax the pressure on the throat.

Then he remembered another pleading pair of eyes that had looked at him. The gersal, he remembered, had been just as helpless under his stick as this man was now under his hands. But given the slightest chance, it would have had its teeth in his leg. And the poison would have poured into his veins. He looked again at Gorham.

His hand tightened and drove downward.

Gorham's eyes widened, then glazed. He gave a half-choked squawk. Feet and body jerked convulsively. Then the hard, taut strength was gone and the man lay limply. Don raised his hand and put his entire weight behind the stroke which drove his extended fingers into the soft part of the man's throat. Then he felt carefully, to be sure there was no vestige of a pulse.

He got to his feet and stood for a moment, looking down at the crumpled figure on the stones. Then he brought his hands up, to look at them appraisingly. He was suddenly aware of a feeling of lightness, of an uncontrollable desire to go into rapid motion. Any motion would do. His muscles simply demanded some sort of violent action. It seemed to him as if he almost floated as he walked over to the book he had thrown as he whirled on Gorham. He bent over and picked it up, then looked about the courtyard.

He turned and looked at the flier.

It was warmed up by this time. He moved swiftly over to it, his body jerking in a peculiar, off-beat cadence as he walked.

As he sat down before the controls, a calm voice echoed in his memory, going through his mind like a cold breeze.

"Let yourself get emotionally involved in a problem and it'll turn around and bite you."

He forced himself to sit back, his hands away from the controls.

Then he looked back at the body on the courtyard paving.

Gorham had implied that he was the power behind the whole present regime. Maybe he'd been bragging. But again, maybe he hadn't. There had been a queer, hard force about the man. There had been an aura which Don had sensed, but could not analyze. One thing was certain. This man had never been able to work under someone else's orders.

He looked around the interior of the flier.

"It's a Royal Guard job," he told himself.

He could see painted legends, giving cautions and instructions to whomever should pilot the ship. He felt under the dash.

There was a light board snapped into clips. He pulled it out and turned on the cabin lights.

Yes, it was all there. Instructions for the identification devices—description of the identification and warning lights. It gave the location of switches—the settings for communications. There was even a small card inserted in a pocket. It gave the communications code used by patrol fliers in routine communication. Don smiled happily.

Now, he could fly back to the hills. It would only take a few minutes, and — —

Why should he? There was an easier way now.

It would be much easier to ride this flier right on into Oreladar. If he headed for the hills, questions might be asked which would be hard to answer. But Oreladar would be the normal place for Gorham to go. And the Federation compound wasn't too far from the Palace. He could feint at the Palace landing pad, then— — He nodded and studied the lighting plan and identification settings.

At last, he nodded in satisfaction, then turned his attention to the small card with the operations code. It was a simple, systematic arrangement, obviously arranged for day-to-day use, not for secrecy. He nodded and clipped it in front of him under the panel light, where he could see it easily. Then, he looked thoughtfully at the courtyard.

There was a small chance that some guard might decide to come into the house, he decided. Of course, it was still to be regarded as a private home, and they had no right to— — He laughed sarcastically.

"That would worry them!" he said aloud.

He got out of the flier and leaned over the body of Gorham. It was surprisingly light. The man had been carrying almost unbelievable strength and power of will in a tiny, frail body. Don threw his load over his shoulder and climbed back into the flier. Then he sat back and looked dully at the control panel.

Suddenly, he felt completely drained. It was just too much effort to get this ship off the ground. And that long flight to Oreladar? Just how much was a guy supposed to do in one day?

He sat supinely for a few minutes, simply staring at a nothingness beneath the surface of the panel. A small noise from the house aroused him, and he jerked up. He'd have to move.

Unwillingly, he pulled at the controls and the flier raised from the paving.

A blast of air hit the side of his face and he turned his head. He'd forgotten to close the door. He snarled at himself in annoyance, then leaned over and jerked at the handle. The ship swayed and dipped toward the lighted streets and he straightened quickly and righted it with a jerk. Then he snapped off the cabin lights and reached down to set up the identification patterns.

A tinny voice snapped at him.

"Rano ninety-one, Riandar control. Seven three seven."

Don looked at the code card before him. Yes, there it was. "Return to station." He glanced at the call sign on the panel before him. He was Onarati three. He nodded. Only an important official would be in this flier. Probably Gorham hadn't been bragging so much.

Another voice had acknowledged the order. Don looked at the speaker grill and shrugged. He set his course southward.

Again and again, the speaker rattled with calls and answers. Riandar control appeared to be busy tonight. Don smiled.

"The busier they are, the better," he told himself. "Then they can't bother me." He coughed.

"Wonder how Korentana made out?" He looked overside.

Abruptly, he was aware of another flier close to his. On its top a blue light blinked glaringly. He looked at it in consternation. Had they — —? But how? He started to pull the control to him and go into evasive flight. Then he stopped.

"Use your head," he advised himself.

He reached out and scooped up the microphone. For an instant, he looked into space, thinking, then he spoke.

"Riandar control," he snarled in an imitation of Gorham's voice. "Onarati three. Got one of your guys on my back. What's the idea?" He released the button.

"Oh, boy," he told himself, "I hope that's the right approach." He looked toward the back of the cabin. If his short contact with Gorham had told him enough, and if he'd judged correctly ... and if Gorham was — —

The speaker crackled. "Onarati three, Riandar control," it said. "Seven zero five?"

Don looked down at the card under the panel light. Yes, there it was. "Give your location."

He mashed the microphone button again. "Seven hundred meters," he snarled impatiently. "South edge of town. Come on, what's this guy doing, riding my tail?"

Another voice intruded into the speaker. "Your pardon, Onarati three," it said. "This is Rano two four. We cannot read your identification lights."

Don looked down at the panel, then shook his head in annoyance. He'd neglected one switch. He reached out and snapped it on. Then he pushed the mike button again.

"So now you happy?" he demanded. "So why ain't ya telling me something, instead of coming around with all them blinking lights?"

The other flier sheered away, its blinker off.

"Your pardon," said the speaker. "We were not sure."

Don sighed in relief. That had been too close for comfort. He glanced down, then blinked and looked again.

"Oh, no!" he growled incredulously. "I left my clothes by the pool."

Kent Michaels opened his eyes. In front of him was a shattered windshield. The light support struts were bent back. The heavy plastic had crackled and powdered. He stared at it. It must have been quite an impact. All he could remember was confused motion, then blackness.

He shook his head to clear his vision, then started to unfasten his seat belt.

And his whole left side exploded as each individual muscle and nerve set up a separate protest. He gritted his teeth against the sharp, red knives of agony.

"Got to reach that belt and get out of here," he told himself. "Wonder how long I've been out?"

He forced his hand to the buckle, then stopped.

"Oh, sure, you idiot," he said aloud. "Go ahead and let the belt go. You can't hurt yourself by landing on your thick head."

He forced himself to ignore the agony in his side and shoulder and looked around the cabin. Evidently, the ship had hit and rolled. He closed his eyes, trying to remember.

He'd evaded the pass that first guy had made at him. Then, when the second one showed up and dove in, he'd gone into a dead-duck spin. So far, so good. Evidently, they'd been fooled. Probably never saw that gag before. But what had happened after that? He searched his memory.

Oh, sure. He'd spun the ship under this overhang and set it down. And the ground had double-crossed him. Even a duck couldn't have kept a foothold on that ledge. He could remember the sudden tilt as the flier slid over and started to roll. Then everything had happened at once. He could remember trying to hold off the windshield from beating his brains out, but— — He opened his eyes. No use trying to analyze that part of it. Things had become confusing.

No matter how you figured it, he was here, hanging upside down in his seat belt in a pretty thoroughly wrinkled up ship. He moved his left arm experimentally.

His side went into screaming agony again.

Well, anyway, the shoulder wasn't broken. It could move—a little.

"Great," he told himself. "Now, how do you get out of this seat belt without breaking your stupid neck?"

He reached out with his right hand, to feel the padded roof under him. Well, maybe he could— — He set his teeth and forced his left hand to the belt release. If he could just hold enough weight with that right hand so that— — Well, no use worrying about it. Something had to be done. He pushed against the release. The shoulder screamed almost aloud. He started levering the buckle apart with his thumb.

Suddenly, the belt let go and he was struggling to put enough power into his right arm to hold himself away from the approaching roof.

For a seeming eternity, he struggled to maintain his balance and ease himself down. Then there was a soft bump. He sank into soft, cushioned blackness.

It was dark when he opened his eyes again. Incuriously, he rolled his eyes from side to side. He could see nothing. He let himself slip back into the soft nothingness.

Slowly, he came back to being. For a timeless instant, he examined a cushion which lay just before his eyes. Then pain messages started clamoring for attention. There were too many of them to unscramble. Everything was screaming at once.

He breathed in shallow gasps, then forced himself out of his cramped position. At last, he managed to get to his knees and crawl out of the gaping hole where a door had been. Outside, he collapsed to the ground and lay, panting.

Slowly, he gathered strength and struggled to his feet. At least, his legs were in working order.

He looked back at the ship, then whistled.

"What a mess! How'd I ever get out of that one?"

He shook his head to clear it, then examined the cave.

The ledge, he discovered, wasn't particularly high. It had just been enough to roll the ship. The slope of the ground and the back wall of the cave had done the real damage. He reached out with his right hand and grabbed a vine. Yes, he could walk himself up the ledge with that. And that would get him out of here.

He turned back and inched himself inside the flier again. The emergency food pack was there. Unbroken, too. He fished it out and opened it, forcing the almost useless left arm to lend a little support as the right worked at the fastenings.

The food concentrate actually tasted good.

It could be a lot worse, he thought. Those two murderers had jumped him only a few kilometers from Kordu valley. Unless he was badly mistaken, this would be Gharu Gorge. It was steep-walled, but it could be climbed. And once he got to the rim, it would be only a days walk to Korelanni.

"Not too bad," he told himself. "Anybody for mountain climbing?"

He got to his feet, reeling a little as his side protested against the indignity of being forced into motion. Probably a broken rib or two, he thought. He brought his right hand over and ran his fingers delicately over the left collar bone, from neck to shoulder. Then, he nodded. It seemed to be in one piece. Might be cracked, but it'd hold together—he hoped.

Slowly, he started pulling himself up the bank, pausing now and then to regain his balance and take a new grip.

Lieutenant Narn Hense gave a snort of irritation, then walked across the guardroom and switched the television off. Those news broadcasts gave him an acute, three-dimensional pain. It was normal, he supposed, for propaganda to sneak into a state-controlled broadcast, but did it have to be so damn— —

"Oh, the devil with it," he said aloud. "I just help run the Security Guard around here. The Commissioner can worry about policy—and diplomatic relations, too."

He glanced at the clock on his desk, then reached out to grab his hat.

"Better take another look at the guard while I'm at it," he told himself.

He strode out of the office, hooking his sidearm belt from a hanger as he went by.

It would be a good idea, he decided, to check post number four first this time. The landing pad guard had been a little less than perfectly alert tonight.

"Probably worrying about last night," he told himself. He smiled reminiscently.

Moresma had been pretty worried and scared when the patrol had brought him in. They'd gotten him out of the jam and kept him out of trouble, but it had been close. The local authorities didn't seem to have much sense of humor when it came to Federation personnel. In fact, they seemed to welcome incidents that could— —

"Funny," he told himself. "There are plenty of Galactics here, too. They get along fine, but let one of our guardsmen drop a chewing gum wrapper— — Oh, well. One of those things, I guess." He walked around the corner of the building and strode down a hedge bordered path.

As he walked, he looked about at the dark Commission buildings. It was a large compound. There were several posts and it took a large security guard detachment to give it adequate protection. He glanced up at the sky.

A blue-lit flier was coming toward him, flying rather low. Suddenly, its lights blinked out.

Hense looked at the suddenly dark shape incredulously. It seemed to be arcing down, toward the compound. He started forward at a run.

Either that pilot was out of control, or he was crazy. In any event, he was going to crash in the compound unless his luck was fantastically good. He'd been coming in fast, too. The lights had indicated an official Oredanian ship.

This, he decided, was definitely irregular.

As he got to the pad, the ship came to an abrupt halt overhead. Then, it came down in a blur of speed. Not more than half a meter from the pavement, it checked its fall and settled. A door popped open.

Hense flipped his light from his belt and snapped it on. The guard, he noted approvingly, had been prompt. The man had dashed up and now stood close by the flier, his weapon at the ready.

A figure came out of the flier and stopped.

"Put out that light!" snapped an annoyed voice.

Hense snapped the switch on his hand light, then stared at the figure by the flier.

Now, what was this? He wasn't accustomed to taking orders from some joker that barged in and shot an unauthorized landing. He was the one who should be giving the orders. He started to raise the light again.

"Leave that light out, hang it," said the voice sharply. "I don't feel like being a target. And you! Don't point that thing at me! Now come on, both of you. Let's get out of the open. Take cover!"

Hense shook his head dazedly. It wasn't right, but there didn't seem to be much room for argument right now. Somehow, that voice carried authority. Moresma hadn't hesitated. He was following the dim figure which ran from the side of the flier. The lieutenant turned and headed for a nearby building. There was a wide overhang there, close to the ground.

Another ship was screaming in, its lights darkened. As Hense dove for cover, brilliant light pinpointed the grounded flier. The guard and the unknown rolled in beside him.

There was a brilliant flash from the landing pad, then a heavy concussion made Hense's chest contract. Lurid flames rose skyward. The attacking flier rose sharply and disappeared. Hense looked after it incredulously.

"Close," commented the new-comer. "Thought for a few seconds I wasn't going to make it. Sure didn't think they'd be with it that fast." He turned and the lieutenant examined him curiously.

Even in the dim light, it was obvious he was pretty young. Khlorisana, as nearly as Hense could tell. Might be a half-caste, of course. But what was he doing here? Why a near crash landing? And who had the eternal gall to pull an attack on a grounded ship right in the Commission compound?

He continued to stare. Come to think of it, what had this joker done with his clothes? Nothing on him but a pair of shorts.

The other noticed the officer's gaze and looked down.

"Yeah, I know." He grinned. "I got busy a while ago. Forgot to put 'em back on. Didn't realize I'd left every rag behind till I was well on my way." He looked at the ground thoughtfully.

"Wonder if they'll trace Korentona through them? Well— —" He faced Hense again.

"I'm Don Michaels," he announced. He held out a large book he had been carrying under his arm.

"Look," he added. "I've brought in something really hot. How about taking me over to see the commissioner? I've got to see him right away."

For more than five years, the ink of First Lieutenant Hense's commission had been perfectly dry. He'd been in one major campaign and he'd served on more than one outworld. For his entire commissioned career, he'd been a Security Guard Officer. And he'd never had a reputation for being at all tolerant when regulations were broken—or even bent.

He looked angrily at the man before him.

"I don't care," he said distinctly, "if you're Hosanna, the Great. What I want to— —"

"Oh, be quiet!" Michaels held up an impatient hand. "I hate to be impolite about this, but it's no joke. I've got something hot here—really hot. I want to see Commissioner Jackson. And when he finds out what I've got, he's going to want to see me. Now let's get over and find him. Move!"

Hense turned and stepped off. This, he decided, wasn't real. He must be dreaming. He tried to stop, but found it was impossible. He'd been given definite instructions, and— —

He walked toward the path to the Residence. Behind him, he heard the newcomer's voice.

"You can go back to your post, guard. Better watch it, though. One of those Royal Guard ships might try a landing. Might be a good idea to get a few more men out there."

Again, Hense tried to turn around and challenge this fellow. Hang it, he was the Officer of the Guard. He was supposed to be giving the orders. In fact, he should have this fellow in the detention cell by now, waiting for the major to see him in the morning. He paused in mid-stride.

"Never mind stopping, lieutenant," Michaels told him. "Just keep going. I want to see the commissioner before Stern's people figure out something really good."

Hense gave up. He must be asleep. It was the only possible answer. Of course, that was bad, too. On some stations, an Officer of the Guard was permitted to take a nap between guard checks. But Major Kovacs had some sort of a thing about that. He'd made it clear that there was plenty of time for napping during off-watch time. His officers, he said positively, would never sleep while their men were on guard.

And he made checks, too. Hense struggled with himself. He had to wake up.

It was insane. How, he wondered, could a guy be asleep and dreaming — and know it? And, knowing it, why couldn't he wake himself up? This was pure fantasy. Yeah, dream stuff. He waited nervously.

Any time now, the major could be coming around to check the guardroom. Then the roof would fall in. Any minute now, he could expect to hear a window-shattering roar.

"Halt!"

It was the Residence Guard. Post number two.

"All right," Michaels' voice was low. "Hold up. Answer him. Have him continue his tour, and let's be on our way."

Hense stopped. "Officer of the Guard," he said loudly.

"Advance, one, to be recognized."

Hense sighed and stepped forward, then halted again at the guard's command.

The man flashed a light on him, then raised his weapon to his face and snapped it to the raise position again.

"I recognize you, sir. Any special instructions?"

"None. Just continue on your post."

Inwardly, Hense was reaching the boiling point. That hadn't been what he'd intended to say, dammit! He— —

"Pardon, sir," the guard was saying, "but how about this man here?"

Now, Hense realized, there must be something really going on. Dream creatures just couldn't walk out of a man's mind and show up in front of an alert guard. Or had he completely lost gyro synch? He— —

Michaels broke in again. "It's all right, guard. Just continue on your post. And keep an especially sharp lookout from now on."

"Yes, sir." The guard snapped his weapon up to his face again, then holstered it and turned to continue his tour.

Hense looked after him.

It wasn't a dream. It was a nightmare.

He resumed his pacing, toward the Residence.

"Oh, well," he thought resignedly, "might as well relax and enjoy it. Wonder what'll happen next."

Commissioner Jackson himself came to the door.

"What was that fire, lieutenant?" he demanded. He noticed Michaels.

"And what have we here?" He drew his head back a little, frowning.

Don interrupted. "Are you Commissioner Jackson?"

"Yes. But— —"

"Good! Here, take this." Don shoved the book out. "And let's go into your office."

Benton Jackson looked incredulously at the figure before him. He reached out and accepted the book, then turned.

"Another of those!" he said softly.

Hense followed them inside. There were, he was discovering, peculiar things about this dream business. He had completed his mission. He hadn't been dismissed. But he could wait here, or he could tag along and see what happened.

"Well, now," he told himself. "Things are looking up."

Jackson walked over to his desk, snapping on the room lights as he passed them. He sat down and placed the book on the desk.

"Well," he demanded, "what's next?"

Don Michaels reached over the desk and flipped the book open.

"Page seven oh one," he said simply. "Read it. Then, I'll start telling you a lot of things." He hesitated.

"You *can* read Oredanian script, I hope?"

Jackson nodded in annoyance. "Of course. Part of my business." He flipped over the pages, looking at numbers. Then he glanced up.

"How about the lieutenant?"

Don faced about. "Oh," he said. "Sorry. You can go back to your guardroom, lieutenant. I'm sorry I had to get rough with you, but I was in a hurry. Still am, for that matter. Only one more thing. For the love of all that's holy, have your people keep a sharp lookout for the rest of the night. I've a hunch Stern's people will try almost anything right now, short of risking full-scale battle."

Hense shook his head dazedly. Jackson looked up from the book.

"It's all right, lieutenant," he said. "Go ahead. And you might take this man's word on the heavy guard. If we've got what I think we've got, and if Stern knows it, he might even risk a battle."

Hense suddenly realized he was no longer under any kind of restraint.

And, he realized, this had been no dream.

He had actually been ordered around like some recruit. And that by some no-good, naked native kid.

His guard had been pushed around. Unauthorized orders had been given to them.

And they'd obeyed those orders—without question.

In fact, the whole compound had been virtually taken over.

And all by this same kid.

And the commissioner said it was all right?

Hense turned away. He'd— —

He took a step, then reconsidered. He had a better idea.

"This place," he said savagely, "has just plain gone to hell!" He stalked through the door.

The commissioner's amused voice followed him.

"Not yet," it said, "but it very possibly might, lieutenant. Don't forget to double your guard."

As the door closed, Jackson looked at Don, a smile wrinkling the corners of his eyes.

"Afraid you were just a little rough on him," he said. "He'll get over it, but it's pretty unsettling, you know." He shrugged.

"But you haven't introduced yourself. Special Corps?"

Don looked at him blankly, then shook his head.

"I'm afraid I don't know what that is," he admitted.

Jackson examined him carefully. "Hm-m-m," he said slowly. "Interesting! Tell me, how long have you been ordering people around like this?"

Don spread his hands. "Why, I don't really know," he said. "You see, I— —"

Jackson held up a hand, smiling. "Never mind. Do you always go around ... ah ... dressed like that?"

Don glanced down, then grinned. "I'm sorry, sir, but I was in something of a dither a while ago. Truth is, I forgot to dress after I— —"

"Wait a minute." Again, Jackson held up a hand. "Start at the beginning. While you're giving me the story, I'll have some clothes brought in for you." He touched a button on his desk, then leaned back.

"All right," he said, "let's have it. First, of course, who are you?"

While Don was talking, an impassive aide brought an outfit for him. He slipped into the clothing as he finished his account.

"So," he concluded, "all we need to do now is to force a conclave and it's all over. From what Gorham told me, I'm pretty sure I can tear Stern apart myself." His eyes clouded.

"Of course, there's Mr. Masterson. I guess they've got him in one of the torture cells."

Jackson waved a hand. "There's no problem about Masterson. We'll have him over here by morning.

"And I have an idea your father is all right. From what you tell me, I'd say he used one of the evasion tricks they teach Guard pilots. Then, he probably made a safe landing." He leaned forward and snapped down the key on his intercom.

"Emergency operation schedule, Lorenz," he said, "as of now. Have the department heads report here immediately. Have Communications get out an immediate message to Deloran Base. I want at least three squadrons, and I want 'em now. Tell 'em to burn the grass." He lifted the switch and turned to Don.

"I'm not going to take any chances from here on," he remarked. "We'll send a squadron of fighters along with you to pick up young Waern and the clan leaders. That way, they'll have protection." He frowned.

"Now, that leaves us with only one more problem."

Don looked up questioningly and the commissioner nodded.

"We'll have to find someone to represent the Waernu before the conclave. And he'll have to be acceptable to the Waernu."

"That's simple. They've already picked me."

"Won't work now. You can bring them before the clans, of course. But they'd be in a hole if you got snapped out on civil charges right in the middle of the conclave."

"Civil charges?"

"That's right. Little matter of that body out in the flier. You know, and I know, the story on that. It's clearly line of duty. But up to the decision of the conclave, you're vulnerable. Remember, Stern can claim Gorham as a police agent. So, you were resisting arrest. Catch?"

"Ow!" Don looked down at the floor. Then he shrugged.

"But Stern has no way of knowing what happened to Gorham."

"Admitted." Jackson smiled. "But he might guess. You'd have to be consulting with his people for some time before the conclave, you know. And he'd have time to figure things out. Here you are. Here's the clan book. But where's Gorham? And Gorham went up to find that book. Adds up, you see."

"You mean I've got to stay under cover from now on?"

"Not necessarily. The clan warden doesn't have to be identified ahead of time. Usually, it's just an honorary job, any way. But this time, he might really have to perform his traditional duty." He looked at Don seriously.

"Remember the private conversation between claimant and prime minister? About that time, the warden is the only protection the claimant has.

"And this is one time a claimant may really need protection."

Daniel Stern slapped a folder down on his desk and got to his feet. He circled the large office, then stopped, looking down at Gorham's vacant desk.

What had happened to Gorham? Papers were stacked all over his own desk. And they should be here. Most of them had been old Jake's concern. He hadn't realized how much detail the old man had controlled.

But where was Gorham? He'd come in from Riandar. Reports showed that much. Then, his flier had suddenly dashed over and landed on the Federation pad. They'd tried to stop him, but— —

Something must have gone wrong up there at Riandar. Something must have made Gorham decide to come back and make a separate deal of his own. But why? There was that pile of clothes in the Waern house. Had he— —?

Maybe that blast had killed Gorham and destroyed his evidence.

He looked around hopefully. It was possible. No effort had been made to restrain him. He still controlled the Ministry. No effort had been made to limit his authority.

He picked up a sheet of paper. Oh, no? They didn't want to limit him — they wanted everything. Here was this demand for a conclave.

And with that Waern kid running around loose, that was bad.

And he had no one to talk to! Of all the people in this palace, not a single one could serve as confidant. With Gorham gone — —

He shuffled through the papers. Yes, here was the formal demand for a conclave. He looked at it unhappily.

And here was the transcript of the Waern claim. It looked too good.

He tossed the papers back to the desk. It was good, and he knew it. He'd seen the originals in the heraldric files. They were destroyed, of course. But here was a photo of that clan book!

And worse, here was the notice from the Resident Commissioner that the claimant had requested protective intervention from the Galactic Federation. That was really bad. He could remember his interview with the commissioner on that.

Jackson had always been something of a problem. He was a stubborn man. But up to now, he'd always backed down — if enough pressure was put on him. This time? Hah!

He'd come in, bringing that rancher — that Kent Michaels. Stern frowned.

Hadn't old Jake said that guy had been shot down — was dead?

He hadn't looked very dead. As councilor of the Waern clan, Michaels was supposed to be calling on Jackson for backing. Who, Stern wondered, was backing who? He recalled the interview.

They'd come in. And he'd started to establish dominance over Jackson.

Then that Michaels had butted in. He was worse than old Jake. What with one thing and another, he'd backed Stern into every corner in the office.

It had ended very simply.

Jackson had simply declared that there would be a conclave.

The Stellar Guard detachment would be in attendance. No irregularities would be tolerated.

And he'd even named the day — today. Then the two of them had walked out.

Stern twisted his chair around viciously and sat down. He punched at a button on his desk.

An aide came through the door. That was another thing. After that fiasco at the Michaels ranch, he'd had to get a new aide. He motioned the man forward impatiently.

"You have made final arrangements for the conclave?"

"Yes, sir. The Heraldric Branch has everything set up. The clans have already gathered in the Throne Room. The private conversation will be held in the Blue Palace. After the conversation, you will escort the claimant across the south lawn, to the Throne Room." The aide half turned.

"I can get you the plan and diagrams, sir."

Stern waved a hand. "Never mind. I've seen them." He paused.

"Now, has my space yacht been positioned back of the Blue Palace? Is it properly serviced?"

The aide paused. "Yes, sir." He looked curious, but said no more.

Stern examined him haughtily. "Very well," he said. "You will remember my instructions. Discuss the yacht with no one. You may go."

He watched as the door closed, then got out of his chair again. It was time for the conversation. He glanced about the office, then went out into the private garden.

As he walked, he looked at the side paths among the trees, which seemed to beckon to ever more enticing vistas beyond. There were the miniature landscapes, with their mountains and lakes. There were the small cottages, where one could sit and enjoy a cooling drink. He smiled wryly and walked across a miniature bridge.

As he reached the other side, he stopped, to lean against the rail. This was not going to be easy to give up.

He watched the water birds for a while, then went on his way.

As he came through a small grove, he saw the yacht. It had been set down where it could easily take off, and yet where it was impossible to see unless one came within a few meters. The aide had done well. He'd have to remember — —

No, he thought, someone else would be dealing with that aide in the future. He'd be long gone.

He walked up to the ship and opened the door, looking inside. Then, he climbed in, glancing at his watch. It was past time for the conversation.

The claimant and his warden would be waiting. So would the other clan wardens, who waited to make up the advance guard of honor.

He wondered how long they'd wait.

He sat down in the pilot's chair and glanced at the gauges. Then he flipped on the view panels and looked outside at the trees.

It had been a lot of fun. But— —

"No use taking foolish chances," he told himself.

He reached for the starting bar, then hesitated.

"Wait a minute," he told himself. "Who's the prime minister around here, anyway? I can— —"

He sat back, thinking. Of course. It was such a beautifully simple idea. Really foolproof. He should have thought of it before.

There would be only the few of them in that private conversation. He should have realized that. They'd present no difficulty. The wardens? He snorted.

Just a bunch of dressed-up idiots. No trouble there. Anyway, only one of them was directly concerned. And he wouldn't really know what was going on. Only the claimant would know. He laughed.

"Wonder just how it feels to get ordered around like that?"

After the conversation, he could walk into the conclave with signed papers. And who would dare challenge that? Even the commissioner's people would have to admit defeat. He smiled. Michaels? He'd be standing there with his mouth open. Nothing he could do. It would be too late.

And once he got that crowd back into his jurisdiction, there'd be no further problems. He'd be sure of that.

This was actually what he'd been waiting for! This was a formal conclave, called at the request of the tribes themselves. They'd have to choose now. And there was no one else.

He, Daniel Stern, would walk out of that Throne Room with the silver robes over his shoulders.

King Daniel!

He climbed out of the yacht and paced toward the small doorway, at the back of the Blue Palace.

He came into the private conference room and walked with dignified stride toward his place. As he came under the canopy, he stopped and placed his hands on the rail.

With haughty appraisal, he allowed his gaze to roam over the men who stood to flank the outer door. At last, he stopped, to center his attention on the two who stood in the doorway.

Here were the two key figures — the claimant and his warden.

The man on the right was dressed as for battle, his polished sling stick shoved into his sash at an angle so as to be easy to his right hand, just to the left of it was thrust the long hillman's knife. There was only one thing unorthodox about his equipment. Stern frowned as he inspected that.

In his right hand, the man carried a long device of wood and metal. Obviously, it was a weapon of sorts. Stern examined it carefully, speculating as to its nature.

It was, he finally decided, some type of beam projector. Judging from the long barrel, it would throw a narrow cone. Mentally, Stern calculated the probable dispersion.

Some Stellar Guard weapon, he thought, that had been loaned to this fellow. Well, it made no difference. Whoever the fellow was, he'd never dare use such a device here. He turned his attention to the other — the claimant.

So this was Pete Waern?

The boy was slight, he noted, even for a native. Definitely, the studious type, decided Stern. He'd present no problem at all.

The regent almost allowed himself a smile. This was going to be easy! He motioned the two forward.

"You have matters for our attention?" he inquired formally.

Waern stepped to the rail.

"I here claim to be the rightful heir to the throne of Oredan," he said slowly. He took a book from under his arm and laid it on the table beside Stern.

"I here present the book of my ancestors," he went on. "In it, at the place marked, is the contract of the last lawful king of Oredan, and of his queen. I was designated to be their son."

Stern nodded. "It is well," he said. "We shall consider this matter."

He opened the book and glanced at the script and the two signature stamps. Then he jerked back dramatically, staring at the book in simulated consternation. He bent forward again, for a closer look.

"This is most strange," he said in a low, wondering tone. He shook his head.

"These looked authentic in reproduction," he murmured. "But now?" He glanced at Pete and was forced to repress a smile.

The expression on the Waern boy's face was perfect. He had him! He looked about the room, then gazed sternly at the claimant.

"I find it almost impossible to believe," he said coldly, "that there is a person in this realm who would have the temerity to bring such a document to my attention for serious consideration."

He stabbed a finger out to point at the book and fixed Pete with an accusing stare.

"I find this a complete forgery," he said harshly. "Your claim is, of course, denied and declared fraudulent." He stepped around the rail, to tower over the boy.

"You will, therefore, acknowledge your crime in writing." He reached out and took a pen from the table.

"You will now write the words, 'forgery, no genuine contract,' over these pages. And you will sign your name." He paused, thrusting the pen toward Pete.

"You will then— —"

The warden stepped forward.

"Pete," he said sharply. "Listen to me!"

Stern looked up in annoyance. The Waern boy had started to take the pen. Now, he stopped and jerked around.

"You will listen to nothing this man tells you," ordered the warden. "You will do nothing he asks. Do you understand that?"

The boy nodded. "Thanks, Don," he said. "He almost got me that time."

Stern glared angrily at the warden.

"You will go back to your place," he ordered. "Do not attempt to interfere again."

Incredulously, he watched as the warden shook his head.

"Sorry, fellow," he heard the man say, "but that doesn't work on me. And it won't work on Pete—not again. Now suppose we do this thing right."

Stern examined the man more closely.

He was larger than the Waern boy, and more strongly built. But he was very little older—and definitely no giant. He was at least fifteen centimeters shorter than Stern himself, and much lighter. Looked, Stern decided, like a galactic. He felt a surge of hatred.

No little man could dare defy him!

He tilted his head a little and looked downward into the warden's eyes.

"Your duties are to protect the person of this boy, so long as he is a legitimate claimant for the throne," he said contemptuously, "not to advise him. Your presence here is merely required by tradition, not by real need."

He smiled coldly. "And, since his claim is obviously nonexistent, you have no standing here. Leave this palace at once!" He pointed imperiously at the door, then turned his attention to Pete again.

"You will write as I told you. Now!"

"Ignore him, Pete." The warden raised his weapon a little.

"Name's Michaels," he told Stern conversationally. "Donald Michaels. You've met my father already." He moved the long weapon again.

"You sent some of your people up to our place a while ago. I destroyed them with this." He jerked his head downward at the barrel of the weapon.

"Brought it along with me when I came down here. It's quite capable of taking you apart, I assure you." He moved a hand on the stock.

"And if you attempt any more of that unlawful coercion," he added, "that's just what will happen. I'll protect my claimant, you see."

He tilted his head, to indicate the other clan wardens.

"These men know what is supposed to be done here as well as you and I," he added. "We all know this is a purely formal meeting. The validity of these documents has already been determined."

"As Prime Minister, I— —"

"It is no part of your duty here to rule on the validity of any document," Michaels interrupted. "And it certainly isn't proper to attempt in any manner to persuade a claimant to abandon his claim. Not here. These things are proper only before the full conclave."

"Are you trying to tell me my duties?" Stern looked incredulous. This was not going well at all!

"I am doing just that," Don told him evenly. "Apparently someone has to." He glanced around the room.

"Are there any other claimants present?"

Stern felt drained of energy. What was this? The father had been impossible to control—like Gorham. Did the son combine other powers with that resistance? Where had these Michaels people come from? He tried once more.

"There are no valid claimants present," he snapped sharply. "I— —"

"That's not exactly what I asked," Don told him. "But we'll take it as meaning that Pete's the only claimant. So, I demand that you follow the ritual and escort him to the conclave." He waved the weapon.

"Come on. We've been held up here long enough. Let's go."

Suddenly, Stern felt powerless. This whole thing had fallen apart. He should never have come in here. He should have just taken off—as he had intended. In space, he would have been safe, at least. Here? He bent his head resignedly.

He could try one more thing. This was a young man—inexperienced. Maybe— —

"You will precede us," he said.

"No," Don told him, "I don't think I will. I think it will be better if I leave that honor to one of the other wardens. I want to be able to see you." He jerked his head at a man who stood to the left of the door.

"Will you honor us, Mernar-dar?"

The other tilted his head. "It is I who am honored," he said. He turned and went out the door.

Dazedly, Stern walked forward, pacing with the claimant. He paused as he got to the porch. Michaels was still standing inside the door.

"Right here," he said coldly, "we shall return to a very old custom. I shall remain, to protect the rear. And I shall watch the entire progress of the advance to the Throne Room." He smiled grimly.

"You are, I suppose, familiar with the range of a medium duty blaster?"

Stern nodded. "I've seen them operate," he admitted.

"Good." Don nodded. "This thing will outrange them a little. I'll have you in my sights all the way. Remember that, and don't do anything that might cause me to fear for Pete's safety."

The wardens spread out, to fan out before Stern and Pete. Acting the part of scouts before a column, they started across the wide lawn, toward the Throne Room.

Stern watched them for a moment, then took Pete's arm. Together, they walked down the long flight of steps. For a moment, they paused at the path, as ritual demanded, for a signal to continue.

Stern allowed his thoughts to race.

There was no question about it now, he thought. This boy would be upheld by the conclave—if he got before it. And if he were now sustained, an ex-regent named Stern would find himself in very grave trouble indeed.

This was much worse than that mob in Tonar City. He glanced toward the gate in the wall ahead and to his right.

Just beyond that door lay his yacht—and safety. If he could only figure out a way——

Across the lawn, a warden was making the signal for the advance. The way, then, was ritually clear. Stern stepped forward, still glancing toward that door.

They would pass within just a few meters of it. Now, where was that Michaels?

Suddenly, he realized he could never hope to get out his hidden weapon, find Michaels with it, and vaporize him. Not until the other had plenty of time to release a beam of his own. He shuddered, remembering the destruction that weapon had caused up in the Morek.

At this range, even the narrowest blaster beam would fan out enough to destroy a man's entire body. And that thing, whatever it was——

Suddenly, he smiled. That was it! It would spread out too much.

He flipped out the little khroal from its hiding place in his sleeve and placed it against Pete's back. With his other hand, he gripped the boy around the throat. Then he turned, seeking to locate Michaels. The fellow was out of sight.

Probably, Stern thought, he had remained in the shadow of the huge pillars of the porch—or even inside the Blue Palace itself.

His whole body itched. The man might fire without thinking! He raised his voice.

"Can you hear me, Michaels?"

He had been right. The answering voice came from the palace doorway.

"I can hear."

"Then listen carefully." Stern put all his persuasive power into his voice.

"I shall not harm this boy unless I am forced to, but I assure you that if I am interfered with, I'll not hesitate. From where you are, you can do nothing. Any blast you release will spread out to kill him as well as me. You realize that?"

"I can hear you." Don's voice was expressionless.

"And," added Stern loudly, "if I am struck or attacked, I will have time to release this khroal. This is also obvious, is it not?"

There was no answer. Stern frowned. What was the fellow doing? He drew a deep breath. He'd have to go through with it now, no matter what.

"I am going to the gate in the wall over there. Shortly after I go through that gate, I shall release this boy, and use a means of escape which I have prepared. You may watch me, of course, but make no effort to stop me — or this boy dies."

He paused again, waiting for an answer.

The wardens, he could see, had stopped and stood, undecided. None of them was close enough to be dangerous.

This, he thought with a surge of hope, was going to work out after all. He turned his eyes for a swift glance at his captive.

Once at the yacht, he could release a bit of energy from the khroal. This boy had destroyed all his careful plans. No, he decided, Pete Waern could not be allowed to live and enjoy those good things the palace afforded.

He tightened his grip about the boy's neck.

Don Michaels had strapped his sling on his arm. Now, he lay on the floor of the Blue Palace. Stern's head was centered in the scope and the cross hairs bobbed slowly about a spot just in front of the man's right ear.

"No question about it," Don told himself, "if Stern gets Pete through that gate, that'll be the end of Pete."

He put pressure on the trigger.

"The guy's as sore as a singed gersal," he told himself. "And half nuts besides. He'll spray Pete with that thing if it's the last thing he ever does." He continued his pressure on the trigger. The cross hairs still hovered about the man's ear.

"Hope that anatomy book was right," he told himself.

Of course, he realized, if he missed the tiny target—if the bullet failed to destroy the motor centers on impact—Stern would die anyway. But he just might be able to press the release on that khroal. And that wouldn't be good.

The aiming point moved a trifle and Don eased back into position.

What had happened to the trigger on this thing? Had he forgotten to take off the safety? Again, the cross hairs started to wander and he eased them back—back toward that little spot.

The rifle leaped upward with a roar, slamming back against Don's shoulder. He let it settle again, examining the scene anxiously through his sight.

Stern was still on his feet, but his hands were dropping limply to his sides. Don could just see the glitter of the khroal by Pete's feet. Then, Stern's knees bent and he flowed to the ground.

Pete had turned at the sound of the shot. He looked back at the palace door, then glanced at the khroal.

At last, he knelt beside the body on the ground. He felt the throat, then examined the man's head. For an instant, he looked a little sick, then he looked away from the tiny hole in front of the man's ear. He got to his feet and waved a hand.

"Pinwheel," he shouted.

The newly enrobed King of Oredan settled back in his chair and shook the heavy cloth back from his shoulder.

"So," he said thoughtfully, "it's all over." He sighed.

"And it's all just beginning, too. Now, I'll have to form a government." He smiled sadly.

"It's funny, Don. For years, I've dreamed of actually being king. Now it's suddenly happened and I feel about as helpless as they come." He stretched out a hand. "All at once, I'm realizing it's pretty rough for a schoolboy to suddenly find himself with a whole nation to run. I don't know where to start."

"You'll get used to it, Pete." Don smiled at him. "Get yourself a few really competent advisors. Tell them what you want, and let them go out and get some competent people to do things. And you've got it whipped."

"Yeah." Pete nodded. "Yeah, I guess that's the way it's done. But— — Well, I asked for it. And they handed it to me." He looked directly at Don.

"How about you? You've got plenty of clan rank, you know. What department do you want?"

Don shook his head slowly. "Don't look at me," he advised. "They offered me a spot in the Stellar Guard and I'm signing up." He glanced around the room.

"I've got no place here."

"What are you talking about?" Pete frowned. "I owe this whole thing to you. I wouldn't even be alive if you hadn't been around. You can have anything you want here, and you know it. What can the Federation offer you?"

Don shrugged. "Oh, I don't know," he said. "Lot of work, of course. Pride of accomplishment, maybe. Peace of mind. Hard to say. Only one thing I'm sure of. I wouldn't work out here."

"I don't get it." Pete shook his head.

Don looked at him, his face expressionless.

"Look, Pete. Do you really like me?"

"Why, of course. You saved my life and set me on the throne. I told you that."

"Not just what I mean. Do you feel perfectly relaxed and easy when I'm around? Would you really call me a close friend?"

Pete squirmed in his chair. Uneasily, he looked overhead at the tassled canopy.

"That's a lousy way to put it," he complained.

"Well?" Don's face was still expressionless.

Pete forced himself to look directly at him.

"I don't know. I ... well, you've done so darn much. Well, I guess I am a little afraid of you, at that." He looked at the floor.

"Oh, all right. I'll have to admit it. You do actually make me uneasy. Always did, even back at school. Lot of fellows felt the same way."

Don stood. "That's what I mean. And it would get worse if I hung around. You'd get so you hated yourself—and me." He held out a hand.

"You're the king—the ruler of this whole nation. That means you've got to be the head man. No one can give you orders. They can suggest, but no one can be even capable of giving you orders." He smiled.

"Dad will rebuild the ranch, of course. And I may come back once in a while, in a very quiet way. But for the most part, I'd better not be around too often."

Pete got to his feet. Suddenly, he looked relieved and at ease.

"I'll make certain your ranch is never interfered with," he promised. "It's yours, so long as you or your father want it. And I hope that some day it'll be a home for your kids." He paused.

"If you ever do decide to come to the capital," he added, "you'll be a welcome guest at the palace."

"O.K." Don grinned. "Let's leave it that way. Good-by, then, and I hope yours is the longest reign in history."

He turned and walked through the curtain.